APPLIED FLOW

APPLIED FLOW

STOP BURNOUT. BE AWESOME.

HEATHER C. INGRAM

NEW DEGREE PRESS

APPLIED FLOW
Stop Burnout. Be Awesome.

ISBN   978-1-64137-934-2 *Paperback*
         978-1-64137-732-4 *Kindle Ebook*
         978-1-64137-733-1 *Ebook*

For

Devon, Layla, Skylar, Elizabeth,
Liam, Dayton, Clay, and Madison

CONTENTS

———

INTRODUCTION TOO MUCH IN A WORLD OF NOT ENOUGH 9

PART I   **PRIMING THE PUMP**   **17**
CHAPTER 1   THROUGH THE LOOKING GLASS   19
CHAPTER 2   GRIT AND FLOW   33
CHAPTER 3   MENTORS AND MIRRORS   41
CHAPTER 4   AN ACCIDENTAL YOGI   51
CHAPTER 5   EMOTIONS. WHAT'S THE POINT?   61
CHAPTER 6   THE SHAPE OF EMOTIONS   69

PART II   **THE FLOW LIST**   **93**
CHAPTER 7   THE FLOW LIST   95
CHAPTER 8   MATCH QUALITY   105
CHAPTER 9   CLARITY   115
CHAPTER 10   FEEDBACK   123
CHAPTER 11   CONTROL   131
CHAPTER 12   FOCUS   139
CHAPTER 13   EVERYDAY LIFE FALLS AWAY   147
CHAPTER 14   SELFLESS   157
CHAPTER 15   TIMELESS   173
CHAPTER 16   LOVE AND CARE   185

PART III	**THE PRACTICE**	**201**
CHAPTER 17	AN UNEXPECTED OUTCOME	203
CHAPTER 18	THE TROUBLE WITH ASSUMPTIONS	211
CHAPTER 19	THE POWER OF PARADOX	227
CHAPTER 20	FLOW BY DESIGN	243
	WHY I WROTE THIS	263
	ACKNOWLEDGMENTS	267
	NOTES	271

INTRODUCTION

TOO MUCH
IN A WORLD OF
NOT ENOUGH

———

Coming out of the 2008 Credit Crisis, Sallie Krawcheck, then a top executive in wealth management, went into her performance review expecting to hear good news. Amid the massive global economic meltdown, she'd risen to the challenge, managing her team through an unprecedented crisis, and basically crushed it.

But instead of receiving praise for a job well done, she received just two pieces of feedback:

"The first was that my work ethic was too strong—it was intimidating and off-putting to the other folks on the leadership team," she recalled in a 2019 interview. "The second was that my profile was too high... I had to pick my jaw up off the table. I said, 'Wait a second. My business results are great. And we're coming out of the financial crisis and you're criticizing me for working too hard?"[1]

She admits that the criticism for being too high profile was especially painful. As a woman, she felt obligated to downplay her personal power, and the suggestion that she was motivated by hubris or ego felt like a personal attack.

I admire the self-awareness and confidence it took to confront that feedback in the moment, correctly asserting, for example, that all the interviews had been done at the explicit request of the firm. Still, she was told, in no uncertain terms, that it was "her problem."

While this is clearly an example of "bad management," you may be wondering,

WHAT DOES THIS HAVE TO DO WITH FLOW?

I'm glad you asked.

Just as we have to get up to get down and there is no light without dark, to understand flow it helps to understand what blocks flow and leads to burnout.

WHAT IS FLOW?

Flow is that peak human experience we get when performing at our full potential and popularized by the research of

---

1   Charlotte Cowles, "The Motivating Power of Staying Pissed Off," *The Cut*, October 23, 2019.

Mihaly Csikszentmihayli.[2] Specifically, it's the feeling we get when we are our most human, awesome, and powerful selves. Abraham Maslow noted that achieving these peak state moments leads to self-actualization.

People describe flow as being "in the zone" or "in the groove." It's the sweet spot that we slip into when we are firing on all cylinders. Steve Kotter of the Flow Genome Project summarizes it neatly with the acronym STER, which stands for Selfless, Timeless, Effortless, and Richness.[3]

FLOW IS POWERFUL

Chemically, when we're in flow, our brain is awash in happy chemicals. Neurologically, we are totally absorbed in what we are doing. This is due in part because our brains are rapidly pulsing between our high maintenance conscious thoughts while simultaneously accessing the full power of our unconscious autopilot brain. Flow by definition is generative, meaning it generates energy, motivation, and enthusiasm. Like an electrical generator it is self-sustaining, and some describe it as invigorating.

It's not a coincidence that flow often occurs when we are in the middle of acts of creation—when we transmute inspiration, spirit, and potential energy into reality.

---

2   Mihaly Csikszentmihalyi, *Flow*, (New York: Harper Perennial, 2008).
3   Steven Kotler and Jamie Wheal, *Stealing Fire*, (HarperCollins Publishers, 2017).

FLOW IS PURE HUMAN

It's what we were made to do if we could do anything. If you watch closely, you'll see that children slip into flow effortlessly on the playground, imagining unseen worlds, building Lego castles, or getting lost in drawing family portraits with pet dragons and dinosaurs. Unfortunately,

WORK IS OFTEN NOT DESIGNED TO SUPPORT FLOW

Many organizations are designed to maximize control and focus. The industrial factory model relies on conformity and in the worst case assumes people function like automatons or cogs. This kind of management blocks people from achieving flow. This in turn creates fear, mistrust, misunderstanding, and carelessness.

Flow is power, and power can be threatening. In the same way thunder and lightning, the roar of a jet plane, the bark of a dog, a protest, or a movement are threatening, our potential power is a force to be reckoned with.

IF FLOW IS PEAK HUMAN, BURNOUT IS DE-HUMAN

This book is both about how we create flow and how we block it. If flow results from the organization of energy, then burnout is entropy, or the disorganization, waste, and blocking of energy. It is the result of frustration, dissolution, and dehumanization.

While you can and should use this book as a productivity hack and resource to achieve your potential, I felt like it was important to contextualize the topic. I couldn't discuss flow without touching on the shadow of discrimination and the ways we unconsciously rationalize dehumanization. Part of the problem is that many of our business models and products are built on exclusion, status, and hierarchy by design.

When products, labor, and our corporate focus are dedicated to differentiation and exclusion, it's no wonder we unconsciously mirror that in the way we manage ourselves and others. Let's face it—this is a natural outcome of our shared human legacy of war, conflict, and survival that we have yet to fully reckon with, much less transcend. Flow is as much about acceptance and owning both our need for survival and our need to thrive, fly, and soar.

I hope this book connects people with their unrealized power and potential by giving them strategies to identify context and the tools to cope and thrive. For those with direct authority and power, I hope it reveals unconscious blind spots. For the record, I also believe we are all in both camps and that most of us have much more power than we realize, much less to tap into. We're not victims, we're Vikings.

I'LL NEVER GET BACK THAT TIME
Dehumanizing, blocking flow, and power issues are not just a "chick thing" or a "diversity issue"—they are power and status issues. Gender and other unconscious assumptions about status just exacerbate these issues, like rubbing salt on a wound.

Even superstars like Google founder Larry Page have experienced the bizarre challenge of being "too good." Former Google executive Kim Scott, in her book *Radical Candor*, recounts Page's experience during one summer internship in which he'd been given a project that would have taken him only a couple of days if he'd been allowed the autonomy to do it the way he wanted.[4]

Even after Page made the business case and detailed the process, his manager insisted that he do it the way it's always been done. So rather than the project taking a few days, it took the entire summer.

According to Scott, the wasted time felt like torture to Page. However, this experience gave Page the empathy and insight into the kind of culture he wanted at Google. Scott recounts one particular conversation in which Page said, "'I never want anyone at Google to have a boss like that. Ever,'... I saw he meant it by the way he led at Google. Larry went to great lengths to make sure bosses couldn't squash their employees' ideas and ambitions."[5]

Take a minute and think about that. We're talking about Larry Page! Larry freakin' Page had to deal with a mindless crappy boss. What would the world be like without Google? What if Page had been discouraged and bought into his manager's shortsighted belief that things were good enough the way they'd always done it?

What if he'd been stuck and held back from creating Google?

The thing is, I believe we are living in that world. There are amazing talented people trapped in organizations, blocked from achieving their potential and accessing flow.

---

4   Kim Scott, *Radical Candor* (New York: St. Martin's Publishing Group, 2019).
5   Ibid.

Part of the reason I choose Sallie and Larry is because they "made it." We love a good underdog story, but only when they win, after they have been anointed and recognized by those in power and the market, or have achieved some other form of social proof.

It's my belief that we are already living in a world where many, maybe even most, people have been blocked and discouraged by myopic bosses. We live in a world where we don't regularly support other people's potential. Most folks need to see it to believe it.

I'd argue that we all have a tremendous amount of power. We all have the power to notice the stars around us, the disengaged, and the brilliant underdogs in our organizations, in our communities, and in ourselves.

MAKING SENSE OF IT ALL

Strap in, y'all. We're going to be going down a rabbit hole discovering the science and psychology of becoming magic. Stepping back and forth between the looking glass, reflecting and refracting the world and our selves.

Not only are we all complicated and mixed-up creatures, but we live in families and societies and work in organizations in an increasingly interconnected world with other folks who are just as mixed-up. It's like a house of mirrors and can get a bit trippy, but the only way through is through—so take a deep breath and prepare to test new ways of thinking and to literally get out of our mind.

I

PRIMING
THE PUMP

CHAPTER ONE

THROUGH THE LOOKING GLASS

What do we do when we don't know which way is up? When leadership tells us we're wrong and yet we know at our deepest level we're right? Making sense of the situation and understanding our context is hard.

Even with the best ideas, the most talented person doesn't always succeed.

When we are not trusted and viewed as outsiders, our strengths work against us. It doesn't matter how invested or loyal we feel or act. When those in positions of power and authority view us as threats, our best qualities can be held against us.

We must learn to recognize and navigate these double binds, catch-22s, and work with leaders and clients who don't always understand how their assumptions and behaviors demotivate and actually create the results they fear.

We also need to understand how to manage our own personal ebbs and flow, and the confidence to know when to push through and when to stop and recharge.

Meditation and metacognition practices help us understand both our external context and inner reality. Building confidence and trust begins with understanding ourselves. Being aware of our body "alerts" teaches us to trust our gut and our intuition. It puts us on a path to becoming aligned with both our intrinsic drivers and extrinsic motivations.

It also sets us up to apply emotional intelligence (EQ) and achieve "Situational Awareness" and a clear understanding of what is really going on. It helps us to pause and keep our cool, even when things tick us off.[6]

Having the right amount of EQ helps us apply the basic principles of game theory in real time and improve our decision-making. The right amount of chill helps us assess our context and whether we are in a cooperative or a competitive situation, so we can respond accordingly.

GET YOUR NERD ON
There are a lot of tools and habits, like meditation and cultivating community and mentors, that can change our lives, even if we don't fully understand why.

---

6   For more on the connection between mindfulness practices and Emotional Intelligence, I urge you to dive into the book *Search Inside Yourself.* Chade-Meng Tan and Colin Goh, *Search Inside Yourself* (New York: HarperOne, 2014).

Most people learn faster when they *feel* the benefits of a practice, so I urge you to try out these ideas on your own. That said, I'm a skeptic and wanted to understand the science. I'll do my best to unpack some of the more woo-woo ideas, connecting them with multiple paradigms from game theory to positive psychology to meditation, neuroscience, yoga, design thinking, and even some linguistics.

It all connects, because everything does!

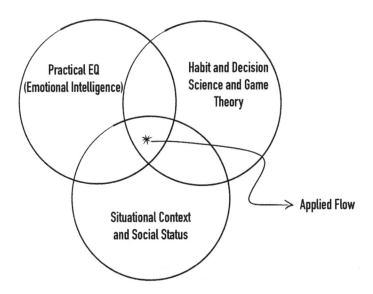

Exhibit 1.1 — Here's a Venn Diagram with lots of nerdy terms. In all seriousness, the model is meant to show how when we align and balance psychology, economics, and decision science, we create a space and channel for flow.

In Part Two: The Flow List, we're going to break down the nine elements of flow. These are the original characteristics that Mihaly Csikszentmihalyi, one of the founders of positive psychology, shared in his original work on flow. The characteristics that define flow can help us create it. More importantly, the Flow List can be used to establish ground rules for our basic entitlements in any organization.

In Part Three: The Practice, we'll get practical with some quick design-thinking frameworks for putting this list into practice. It's going to be a rough ride; you may have to Google some stuff. I have faith in you, and anyway...

Life's too short to not be awesome.

FLOW TOOL: THE X-BOX

The "X-Box" is a tool I use to make sense of the world. It's a form of Johari Window mixed with the prisoner's dilemma windowpane analysis. The idea behind it is to quickly unpack disagreements or misalignments and help us understand when our view or assessment about risks and probability don't match with those of others.

Table 1.1 – General X-Box

	Perception B—Disagree	Perception B—Agree
Perception A—Agree	B. Dissonance	A. Agreement
Perception A—Disagree	D. Disagreement	C. Dissonance

In general, when there is a "tie"—when there is dissonance (i.e., when boxes B and C in the example above don't line up)—it defaults to D. Disagreement.

We can simplify it even further by thinking of it as a variation on the game of tit for tat—which is like being on a seesaw that has many different cycles—where the "power" shifts between each of the two parties.[7]

Table 1.2 – General X-Box

	I DON'T TRUST	I TRUST
YOU TRUST	B. Short Term: YOU LOSE / I WIN Long Term: You Don't Trust so we default to box D	A. WE ALL WIN And live happily ever after—or until the next time we play.
YOU DON'T TRUST	D. WE ALL LOSE	C. Short Term: YOU WIN / I LOSE Long Term: I Don't Trust so we default to box D

For those unfamiliar with the concept of tit for tat, I recommend checking out https://ncase.me/trust/, which is a terrific interactive primer.

APPLYING THE X-BOX TO SALLIE KRAWCHECK'S STORY

Krawcheck assumed she was in Box A—the "we're all in this together" box. Krawcheck learned the hard way that she was competing with both her organization and leadership team in a zero-sum competitive game—i.e., Box C. In those kinds of environments, we are not trusted. Our success is someone else's loss and vice versa. If we are seen

---

7   For accessible business books on game theory, check out *Thinking in Bets* by Annie Duke, *Barking up the Wrong Tree* by Eric Barker, and *Give and Take* by Adam Grant.

as a threat and not as a member of the in-group, it doesn't matter how well we perform. We won't be allowed to rise because the leadership will always come up with a rationalization for their distrust.

	Krawcheck Doesn't Trust	Krawcheck Trusts
Bank Trust		A. Krawcheck assumed she was playing as a trusted team player.
Bank Doesn't Trust	D. Result: Leadership has hidden rules and standards. Does not trust and eventually excludes Sallie.	C. "That's your problem." Krawcheck is disempowered and put in her place and also realizes her mistake and moves to Box D.

APPLYING THE X-BOX TO LARRY PAGES'S STORY

In Pages's case, he dove into his summer internship like many other eager beaver overachievers. I imagine Page was excited to get real world challenges in which to apply his brain and skills. Instead, he was met with insecurity and mistrust.

Not since Julia Roberts swanned into a boutique on Rodeo Drive, with her hands full of designer shopping bags, have the words "Big Mistake—Huge" been better applied.

	Page Doesn't Trust	Page Trusts
Boss Trust		A. Page recommends a really good and efficient solution.
Boss Doesn't Trust	D. Result: Boss missed out on having one of Google's co-founders "owing" him.	C. Manager, whether through insecurity or laziness, doesn't trust Larry's idea and is unwilling to try it. Blocks Larry for proving the elegance of his solution. Larry moves to Box D.

DON'T WASTE TIME MAKING SENSE OF THE IRRATIONAL

"My mother was very strong about my doing well in school and living up to my potential. Two things were important to her and she repeated them endlessly. One was to 'be a lady,' and that meant conduct yourself civilly, don't let emotions like anger or envy get in your way. And the other was to be independent."

—RUTH BADER GINSBURG[8]

We waste a lot of time stuck in frustration and anger. In my opinion, Ruth Bader Ginsburg is the epitome of class. Reading her biography, we realize that her mother taught her that manners included a form of mindfulness and reserve. It was from her mother that she became aware of how focusing on injustice and anger are counterproductive.

---

8   Ruth Bader Ginsburg et al., *My Own Words* (Simon & Schuster, 2016).

It is *mostly* a waste of time to remain angry, or to attempt to parse bullying from gender bias. Unfortunately, this is a lesson I learned the hard way, as I struggled to make sense of the mixed messages I was getting from a new boss and team, in an environment that was increasingly toxic and unwelcoming.

Having coached and mentored other folks since then, I now know it's natural to want to make sense of our situation and find the lesson in the trauma. At the time I wish I knew how to...

SKIP THE BULLSH*T.

By definition, we cannot make sense of the irrational.

Unfortunately, we can get stuck and fixated on the belief that we need external validation—the gold star from our bosses and clients. In my situation, it was a waste of effort—no matter what they thought about me. My new boss and team were simply not trustworthy. I neither trusted nor respected them, which is why I was never going to get their gold star approval in the first place.

It's a bit like being annoyed and hurt when a jerk dumps us. Rejection sucks but come on—we knew it was gonna happen, and it's silly getting upset just because someone else pulled the trigger first. Just say, "thank u, next."

Here's something that took me way too long to figure out: happy, self-actualized people are too busy being awesome to bother being a**holes.[9] Not only are self-actualized people happier, they are more productive and more likely to bring out the best in others.

Basically, don't waste time with jerks; life's too short not to be awesome.

DOUBLE BINDS: NOT JUST FOR THE LADIES

A good deal has been written about the dizzying contradictory feedback and messages women get. Frankly, I'm too tired and over it to repeat it all.

The short of it is dealing with this kind of bullsh*t feels like a catch-22 or a double bind—we approach the glass ceiling only to have the goal posts moved, or when we are offered mixed feedback like "you're too aggressive" or "not likeable" and also "too soft."

I know. We are ALL so over it.

In his 2016 TEDTalk, "How to Speak up for Yourself," Professor Adam Galinsky reminds us that the double bind is not just about gender or bias, it's about status and power. Or as my dad, a gruff surly old white man who worked construction all his life, would say, "He who has the gold makes the rules." In other words, rich people can do what they want.

---

9   Dr. Wayne W. Dyer and Deepak Chopra, *How to Get What You Really, Really, Really, Really Want* (Hay House, 1998).

FLOW IS POWER.

My microeconomics professor, Sharon Oster, an overall badass and the former acting dean and professor emeritus from Yale School of Management, reminded us that our value can be categorized into three Ws: work, wisdom, and wealth. The source of all three is flow. Flow produces work, creates wealth and wisdom, and is also a product of work, wealth, and wisdom.

Many of us have been taught to be humble, to not acknowledge our power directly, and to not threaten those with direct authority or power. Left untapped or unacknowledged, we can forget we have power. Some competitive bullies take advantage of this void, claiming this unacknowledged power and in some cases actively devaluing others to "keep folks in their place."

If we can't hold such folks accountable, we can at least do our best not to give them any more time or energy than we must.[10]

MILQUETOAST AND BASIC ADVICE

A lot of advice we get is unilateral—that is to say, one-sided.

- Buckle down and focus
- Toughen up and develop a thick skin
- Be so good they can't ignore you
- You can change the rules when you get to the top

---

10 Robert Sutton in his book *The No Asshole Rule* defines an "asshole" as someone who has the power to cause harm, denigrate, or de-energize someone else with less power. Robert Sutton, *The No Asshole Rule* (Business Plus, 2010).

These rules are based on what works for the majority of people, folks who think in the default or normal way. Looking back, it seems obvious now, but all that advice and training we got was geared toward average, young, rich dudes who wanted to be average, old, rich dudes.

General advice often works for "normal" people who don't want to push the boundaries, test limits, or color outside the lines. It generally works because they don't need to rock the boat by creating something new. They are safe and cozy, like Chris Evans in a sweater. This is not intended to be a dig in anyway. Have you seen Chris Evans in a sweater? Magical.

If we are different, an outlier in any way, standard advice doesn't cut it.

STATUS, CLASS, AND QUESTIONING THE RULES

Yes, he's an old white man and, in some ways, problematic, but I do love sensible Warren Buffet advice.

Those of us that grew up as part of the working class were brought up with the belief that we had to "pay our dues." Warren Buffet once pointed out that the idea of paying dues in a job you don't love is like waiting to have sex until your old age.[11] Bonkers!

If successful rich people acknowledge this wisdom, why do working class folks still admonish their kids to stay on track

---

11 Marcel Schwantes, "Warren Buffett Says This Career Advice Is All Wrong," *Inc. Magazine,* January 28, 2019.

and play it safe in the corporate industrial model of work? I've seen the result of this narrow perspective and it has led to an increasing division between the wealthy and everyone else. It's senseless.

Buffet himself acknowledged this in a *Washington Post* interview: "there's been class warfare going on for the last twenty years, and my class [the rich] has won." I get the sense that he would like to see upward ability linked more closely to merit. One way to do that is to correct the myth that wealth and status can be attained with just hard work.

Wealthy "upper-class" people don't trade their time for money. They don't buy in to the myth of mindless tenacity. They understand that one doesn't hold on to investments past the point of diminishing returns. They also understand that there is such a thing as being too gritty and tenacious chasing bad investments and sunk costs.

Of course, defying convention and refusing to do pointless work can come across as "difficult," "arrogant," and "lazy." That notion is worth unpacking.

Successful people quit all the time. When they do it successfully, they call it "pivoting" or "iterating." Successful people say sh*t like, "You never fail, you just learn." Don't believe me? Check out Instagram or Pinterest, people love to repost inspirational quotes.

The problem with internet inspiration is it's all cognitive, meaning it sits in our head but goes nowhere. Success, especially creative success, requires us to leave our comfort zone, or at least our couch, at to take action. We have to risk our time, energy, or money.

Successful people are often big losers. They just happen to be bigger winners.

CHAPTER TWO

GRIT AND FLOW

———

TWO SIDES OF THE SAME COIN

When I talk about flow, some folks assume it's all sunshine and unicorns and that the desire for flow is for entitled young people who don't want to do "real work." The implication is, of course, that I'm one of those slackers. They see my Ivy-League pedigree and assume they know my story.

Rarely do they assume that I've been working since I was fifteen; that I paid my own way through college and business school, taking on loans, work-study, and debt; that I spent summers working dirty and menial jobs; or that I've paid my dues on the bottom rungs of the corporate ladder, hustling and tolerating my share of sexism and exclusion.

These assumptions used to piss me off. It took me a long time to understand that it was rarely about me. It wasn't about what I did or did not do. It was a reflection of them.

These days, my literal job is to help people make sense of their culture and to question their assumptions. I help them question the belief that work has to suck and provide tools and training so that they can break the wheel![12]

Flow is not lazy. In fact, "grit" is a big part of the process of achieving flow. In Angela Duckworth's book *Grit*, flow and the elements of flow are interwoven into her narrative. Duckworth writes, "Gritty people do more deliberate practice and experience more flow. There is no contradiction..."[13]

Boom!

Grit and tenacity enable practice, and it is practice with feedback that creates moments of transcendent performance. Ample research shows that deliberate practice enables mastery and excellence. In addition, grit paragons, from the swimmer Michael Phelps to soccer superstar Mia Hamm, demonstrate match quality, a key element of flow. Underlying many of the grittiest stories in Duckworth's book are elements of care, love, and support from family and community—in other words, the elements that make up flow!

---

12   Is it too soon for a *Game of Thrones* reference? Hodor!

13   Angela Duckworth, *Grit* (Vermilion, London, 2017).

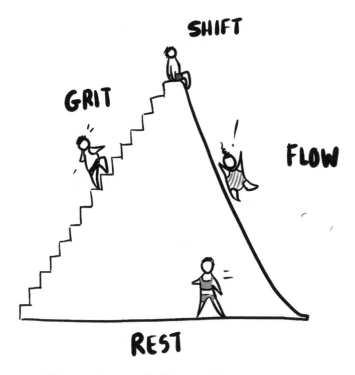

Exhibit 2.1 — If we imagine flow like a water slide, we can break it down into all four phases: Grit, Shift, Flow, and Rest.

Grit is only part of the human process. We also need to understand and teach when to shift to get into flow. Finally, we need to know when to rest and recharge. Notably, resting and recharging is often the most overlooked and underrated part of the process.

GETTING INTO FLOW REQUIRES A BALANCED APPROACH TO MOTIVATION

A lot of this book comes down to figuring out our balance and often requires us to hold on to both sides of the equation.

Successful and happy people tend to question false binary choices and refuse to pick a side. Instead of "either or," they elect for "both and." They intuitively transform the milquetoast advice from earlier into things like:

- Buckle down and focus AND relax and explore
- Toughen up, develop a thick skin AND set boundaries where you can be empathetic
- Be so good they can't ignore you AND stop hustling to prove your worth
- You can change the rules when you get to the top AND be a leader and ally from day one

TANGO ON

"No mistakes in the tango. Not like life... that's what makes the tango so great. If you make a mistake, get all tangled up, you just tango on."

—AL PACINO, SCENT OF A WOMAN.

I think that life and the tango have more in common than Al suggests. Life is messy. Success comes from a mix of luck, talent, and effort. Sometimes success happens when the rules are followed and sometimes it occurs when we defy convention.

A lot of well-meaning "experts" claim to know the secret of success. I'm skeptical that they know any more than what worked for them at that time, and that their success was based on anything more than luck. The one thing I do know is we have to be in it to win it—we have to tango on. Successful people keep showing up; they keep investing their time, their effort, their insight, their money, their assets, and their energy. The one and only thing all successful people have in common is that they keep playing until they win.

They have faith and keep up their energy to endure. Success is inevitable as long as we keep learning, improving, and never ever giving up.

Or we die trying. J

GRIT, FIT, AND FLOW

"As much as talent counts, effort counts twice."

—ANGELA DUCKWORTH, GRIT

Anyone who has played sports knows that talent only goes so far. Talent is the starting point. Talent may make it fun to start and it may even give us a leg up, but it won't take us to the top. Successful athletes have what Carol Dweck defines as a "growth mindset."

If we stick with something long enough, we learn to love the process. We lean into the good things, meeting our teammate at the track, bonding over our shared hatred of 400s. We learn to appreciate the ache of muscles after a tough workout, the gradual gains in endurance, the ability to push just a bit harder, and the rewards of hanging a bit tougher on game day.

> "I've always believed that if you put in the work, the results will come."
>
> —MICHAEL JORDAN

Playing and cheering on New York ultimate teams, there's one cheer that never fails to fire me up.

Caller: NEW YORK!

Sideline: DO WORK!

New York! Do Work! New York! Do Work!

Again and again, each step, grind, do work, grind, do work. All we can control is ourselves. On the field, cleats digging into the grass, sweat, bruises, aching muscles, grass stains, and abrasions—evidence of the grind and work. We do it all for those rare moments of transcendent connection with our teammates when a play comes together.

For almost two decades, this was my happy place.

The practice, the track workouts, and doing the work just made winning even more satisfying.

One friend who never played competitively said playing frisbee sounded more like a job than fun. I recalled that comment in a particularly fierce game during regionals up in Devens, Massachusetts. I was sweaty, tired after a marathon upwinder, where we had just taken half before securing a spot to Nationals.

"Good job," Ali, my captain, said, patting me on the shoulder.

My heart swelled. F**k yeah, I thought. It was my job *and* it was fun. I wasn't thinking—I was just doing. Hell, it was better than fun. Screw fun. Grit wasn't what kept me playing after two ACL tears. I did it for the flow, my team, and the love. Grit was just the price of admission, but flow was the main attraction. It was where I fit in and belonged.

"Fit can be mistaken for grit," David Epstein, journalist and author of the best-selling book *Range*, commented on a podcast.[14] Flow is the ultimate expression of fit. Grit prepares us for flow, but flow may be the reason we grind.

Paying our dues in a lower tier job should not be confused with deliberate practice or refining one's craft as an apprentice to a master. To get better, we have to practice and do the work. Gaining access to certain opportunities to learn may require scut work and checking our ego. However, we must be certain when paying dues that we fully understand the costs and benefits—weighted by our best guess as to whether we'll be able to collect.

We cannot blindly trust that our boss or organization won't take advantage of us or even know what they are doing. Let's face it, many bosses are also stressed and burned out, unable to take care of themselves much less those they manage.

We must be our own leaders.

---

14   Mark Shapiro (host), "David Epstein on Match Quality, Burnout, & Range," Explore the Space, 146, August 22, 2019.

CHAPTER THREE

MENTORS AND MIRRORS

"The first defense against a culture that hates you is a person who loves you. Love is the most powerful and underused force for change in the world."

—MELINDA GATES[15]

There are many ways to gain perspective and grow into our awareness and wisdom. We do this by reflecting internally and through the reflections of those we trust. We need this awareness to move forward in life, with energy and confidence. To act with confidence, it helps to understand the rules, the players, whether we're playing for the long term or short term, the invisible rules, who to trust, when to pivot, and when to stick.

Winning a game that we don't understand is just luck. It happens, but it's not repeatable. For some, life has been set up by their family and society to ensure that they don't fail.

---

15 Melinda Gates, The Moment of Lift (New York: MacMillan Audio, 2019, Chapter 4).

In Part Three, we'll dig in a bit more about "resulting" and the difference between luck and bias.

We're not taught this out of the gate because early on in our career, we're better off taking action. Understanding the rules only becomes necessary when we hit a wall and get diminishing returns that don't match expectations. This happens more often when we push beyond the average and work to create something new. That's when we face psychological resistance, both from within ourselves and mirrored by others. The trippy thing is just because this resistance is imaginary doesn't mean it's not real.

To overcome it, we may have to

GET A BIT META

Metacognition, or "mindfulness," seems to be the "hot new thing," which is funny since it's based on a millennia of tradition. What is clear is that we need it now more than ever. In our stressed-out, twenty-four/seven, always-on lives, we turn off our cell phones more than we turn off our brains. That's a problem, considering the only time I power down my iPhone is when it crashes. Don't judge me—I know I'm not the only one. Many of us have lost the ability to step back and pause. It's from the pause that we learn to observe, listen, relate, and connect.

Hitting the reset on our brain and resting is an essential part of the cycle for achieving peak performance. The ability to hit pause and step back is essential for not just excelling at what we do but making sure we are playing the right game from the start.

We get stuck playing the wrong game or working for the wrong people or organization. If we are not careful, we can get stuck and worn down. This is especially true if we focus on the unfairness or if we lose perspective of our long game. Losing sight of our vision and losing faith blocks our flow. However, the right insight at the right time can make all the difference. When those insights come, we still have to be open to receiving the lesson and doing the work.

EVEN THE BRIGHTEST STAR CAN BURN OUT

"I was so busy playing the game, I'd forgotten why I was playing."

—LESLIE ODOM, JR.[16]

Not long before his star turn as Aaron Burr in the Broadway hit musical Hamilton, Leslie Odom, Jr., thought very seriously about giving up acting. At the tender age of twenty-nine, he'd already achieved a level of success that most only dream of, and yet success still *felt* a lot like failure.

At the time, he was getting solid work on television, but it was grinding him down. Despite talent, dedication, hard work, and even luck, he had failed to achieve the level of success he dreamed of. In his memoir *Failing Up*, he described it as

---

16   Leslie Odom, Jr., Failing up (Feiwel & Friends, 2018).

feeling heavy, almost depressed. His heart was battered and bruised, guarded and tight, and his shine was gone.

In other words, he was burning out.

A LOVING KICK IN THE PANTS

It is a rare miracle to find someone who wants our success as much as we do, and also who can hold us up and advocate for us. Odom credits a large part of his superstar success to having Stuart K. Robinson as a friend and mentor. Having the benefit and perspective of someone who's farther along the path and willing to share the unspoken and invisible rules ahead is priceless.

Odom didn't need someone to tell him that Hollywood is biased and that tokenism is real, sh*ty, and painful—he'd lived it all his life. Robinson knew Odom had every reason to quit what is a nearly impossible business. It was the rational thing to do. Hollywood is not fair and is notoriously dehumanizing for the very best and even the most privileged.

Still, Robinson could see Odom's potential and, more importantly, knew how to help him realize it. He didn't mince words when he told Odom,

"BEFORE YOU GIVE UP, I'D LIKE TO SEE YOU TRY."

Those words from his mentor's mouth felt like a punch in the gut. Already a seasoned pro, Odom was no stranger to hard work. Robinson knew that, and still pushed him.

"What are you doing when you're not working? What are you doing to make the phone ring?" he asked, throwing down the gauntlet, "Are you singing, are you learning, are you growing?"

Odom could have resisted and responded with a million rationalizations but instead, he listened. It turned out to be the spur he needed to get out of his rut. In retrospect, he admits, Robinson's advice was so obvious it was embarrassing.

I've seen this pattern over and over. Many of my clients get caught playing the game by other people's rules, and in so doing get stuck, frustrated, and angry at a corporate system that has the same odds as an Atlantic City slot machine— with just enough random wins to be addictive. It's what keeps the hopeful working-class suckers—the rubes—buying in.

Eventually, Odom sucked up his pride and tried something new. He signed up for Robinson's beginner class for commercials. That's how he found himself in a classroom of fresh off the boat noobs—the kind of starry-eyed LA transplants that they tell stories about. From the start, he knew he did not belong. He was a professional, a veteran of Broadway, and a graduate from a top conservatory with the slick polish to prove it.

Indeed, this "polish" really came through during the first exercise, when Robinson asked the student to introduce themselves in front of the camera. Odom recalls watching how the rookies fumbled, awkwardly answering questions. Unlike them, Odom answered with the self-assurance of a true pro. He was certain he nailed it, until Robinson played back the recordings—without the sound. Reviewing the footage, it became abundantly clear to Odom just how wrong he'd been.

As the recording played, Robinson informed the class that sometimes audition tapes are reviewed without the sound. He explained casting agents look for energy, an unspoken, indefinable spark.

Watching his forty-five seconds play back, Odom saw that he seemed to have "a film of corrosion and jadedness." His spark and his love for the craft was gone. It was clear how the years of being a professional had taken their toll.

That spark is our energy. It's the jolt we get when we are in the flow. It is the potential of all the unrealized needs and desires that humans are uniquely able to sense, realize, and channel. It's our gift and our purpose.

Odom was losing faith and, with it, his love. Robinson's prodding helped him see this. After that, Odom made a decision. "I made a commitment to myself to come rushing forward into the rooms I was invited into, no hanging back, no waiting to find out if it was safe."[17]

TAKEOFF: MASTERING THE SHIFT AND PIVOT

What Odom accepted in that moment was that grit, hard work, and talent are the price of admission. They are essential elements to almost any successful endeavor, but they can only take us to the top of the mountain.

---

17 Leslie Odom, Jr., *Failing up* (Feiwel & Friends, 2018).

To soar, we need enough power to take off and defy gravity. We must master the pivot, knowing when to shift from grinding into flow.

The first key to mastering this shift or pivot is being aware of when we are getting diminishing returns. With practice we learn when we need either pause and take a breath, or when we need to shift to high gear and launch.

This is where the power of reflection comes in. We cultivate mirrors, internally through mindfulness and externally through our relationships with a mentor, coach, or friends. Understanding when to pivot is not a matter of intellect. More often than not, it's a feeling, a gut clinch, an ache beneath our breastbone, that shaky hesitancy, or a heavy stubbornness that grips us.

We can learn how to recognize these inflection points by ourselves.

However, when we're in the middle of the storm it is hard to pause.

Focusing on the work, doubling down on what we already know, and being gritty often feels right and good. This is especially true for high achievers at the beginning of their careers who identify strongly with being gritty and tenacious. We pour ourselves into channels that aren't wide enough to hold us, pushing past our frustration. We give until we have nothing left, not even enough reserve energy to get back up, which can leave us burnt out and empty.

TAKING CARE OF OUR ENERGY IS OUR JOB

"My literal job is to maintain my mental health."

—ELIZABETH GILBERT[18]

Creating anything new takes energy, focus, and courage. We can do it alone, but like mirrors in a lighthouse, when other people are aligned with our energy and vision, they amplify our energy. That is a gift a great mentor and teacher can provide.

TRANSFORMATION TAKES POWER

"Learn the rules like a professional so you can break them like an artist."

—ATTRIBUTED TO PABLO PICASSO

"If you don't know it's impossible, it's easier to do. And because nobody's done it before, they haven't made up rules to stop anyone doing that particular thing."

—NEIL GAIMAN[19]

"Stop following the Old Rules, which exist only to maintain the status quo. If we follow the rules we've always followed, the game will remain the same. Old ways of thinking will never help us build a new world."

—ABBY WAMBACH[20]

---

18 Elizabeth Gilbert, @elizabether_gilbert_writer, July 25, 2019, Instagram.
19 Neil Gaiman, University of the Arts Keynote Address, 2012, May 17, 2012.
20 Abby Wambach, WOLFPACK (MacMillan Audio, 2019).

For creative underdogs, the status quo is not in our favor—we have to create our own path. Companies claim they want the best and brightest to come forward with their full energy and potential. Unfortunately, many companies are better set up to control and limit that energy. One senior management consultant admitted in a rare moment of candor, "there just isn't enough room at the top."

It's an open secret that those at the top need followers, drones to work. It's a pyramid scheme. There are too many people who want to be architects and not enough bricklayers to do the work.

We may be forced to start by playing the hand we are dealt but it is foolish to continue to play a game that is rigged against us.[21]

Leslie Odom, Jr., kept going because of his mentor and eventually succeeded, but not through the old Hollywood system. He's a household name, in large part because he hung in there, committed to his energy, honed his craft, and *leapt* at the opportunity to be a part of the brilliant, innovative, and

---

21 Note: Sometimes when we refuse to play the default games, those who see themselves as better than us may accuse us of being lazy, arrogant, elitist, and entitled. They may get angry that we are not buying into the system and refusing to stick around to prop them up. This may hurt, but it's not a reflection on us. They need us, but they also don't want to give us what we need. Basically, it's a failed negotiation and it happens. We all have a rare and priceless gift. There will always be people who, even though they can't afford our gift, will demand we sell it to them, they feel entitled to our attention and time. It is not mean, or unkind of us to limit the time we spend with trifling hustlers who don't respect us. It is not our job to enlighten them, educate them, or even convince them that we are worthy of respect. Respect is sine qua non!

amazing production of Hamilton, with its color-conscious casting and blend of musical styles that pushed boundaries and elevated the art form.

In doing so, he soared and helped show the world that there was demand for people like him to tell new and better stories. In other words, he changed the game.

CHAPTER FOUR

AN ACCIDENTAL YOGI

———

"There is a difference between knowing the path and walking the path."

—MORPHEUS, THE MATRIX

Not all of us are blessed with a mentor to reflect our life back to us.

Not all of us listen to wise folks when they do appear in our lives.

Some of us, knuckleheads, have to learn everything the hard way.

No one is more surprised than I am that I'm teaching meditation, acceptance, and self-compassion. I'm not a guru or even particularly Zen. The truth is, I'm a class-A, bona fide try-hard. Also, I'm skeptical of the cult of positivity, and smug, clueless folks who are super impressed by their self-awareness.

So, how did I get here? Sheer stubbornness. By working on myself, I've learned that if we don't learn a lesson the first few hundred times, the universe will gladly keep smacking us in the head until we get it.

THE CRISIS

I *knew* about the benefits of mindfulness long before I committed to the practice. But like my bike, which I've used exactly ten times, that knowledge collected cobwebs.

I was a slacker when it came to making it a regular practice. I resisted taking my foot off the accelerator, especially when I found myself working with in a hyper-competitive team of consultants with a new partner who explicitly told me to work harder and faster.

I could *feel* how I was being judged both on my work and my ability to fit in, even while I felt increasingly disconnected. During that time, I learned why management consultancies are often referred to as "burn and churn" factories.

This happened at the same time that I decided to learn more about yoga and meditation. I'd gotten certified to teach yoga almost on a whim. After the third surgery to repair my torn ACL, I was reluctant to get back on the field. Yoga was one of the few things I could do that made me happy. Curious about why yoga felt so good, I figured learning how to teach it would deepen my practice. That intuition was right on. Almost from the first day, I learned that yoga and meditation are two-thousand-year-old wisdom sciences designed to teach people how to be happy and find flow!

I started to practice more often but not daily.

The paradox of mindfulness is that those that need it the most often have the most difficulty doing it. I was doing well enough. I was good but not great. But, really, who was happy? Certainly no one I worked with was happy. I was fine. I was surviving.

Then I found myself in one of the worst situations imaginable.

LEARNING TO LISTEN

"Between stimulus and response there is a space. In that space is our power to choose our response. In our response lies our growth and our freedom."

—ATTRIBUTED TO FRANKLIN COVEY BASED ON
HIS INTERPRETATION OF VIKTOR FRANKL'S
EXPERIENCE IN MAN'S SEARCH FOR MEANING

Looking back, the whole thing couldn't have lasted for more than twenty minutes. At 7:04 a.m., M.E. Swing's, my morning coffee spot, had been open just long enough for me to get a cup of coffee. That was when we heard what I assumed were firecrackers.

"Isn't it a little early?" Tony joked from behind the counter as he pulled a shot of espresso. I rolled my eyes in agreement. Independence Day was still a month off, but there were always a few yahoos who couldn't wait.

Settling down to write, I gazed out the big glass windows, looking for inspiration outside my laptop. That was when I noticed something odd about the parked car on the street in front of me.

Was that a crack? Or a...

"Get down!" I shouted. It was a hole, a bullet hole. "I think that's gunfire!" I yelled as I crouched under the table. Why was I equivocating? That was *definitely* a bullet hole.

"That's gunfire. Get down! Get down!" I repeated. Everyone seemed to be moving in slow motion. My thoughts flashed back to the summer when the city was terrorized by the DC sniper. Swing's, with its huge glass garage doors, was basically a fishbowl—a perfect shooting gallery.

Huddled under the table, I dialed 9-1-1 and eventually ran to the back room with the other staff and patrons. On the phone with the operator, I eventually peered out one of the shop-front windows where I could see a shoot-out in the YMCA parking lot across the street. Two men were behind a black SUV—one injured on the ground, one engaging an unseen assailant.

Much later, I learned they were congressional police, but at the time I didn't know if I was watching a gang war or terrorists. I watched as the first Alexandria police officer arrived and engaged with who I now know was the shooter.

In between punctuations of gunfire, people ran across the basketball court, like gazelles fleeing a lion on the Serengeti.

In front of me, just outside our precarious viewing perch, two kids used my own red Altima for cover.

I didn't know that three days later, I'd returned to the crime scene to allow an FBI agent to collect a bullet embedded in my car. But that was long after.

AFTER THE ALL CLEAR
After the pop, pop, pop ended.

After the helivac came and took away the wounded congressmen and police.

After we all emerged, dazed from hiding.

After endless scrolling through social media and the news.

After we learned what had happened.

After I gave my statement.

After,

We were all told the coffee shop was closed. We had to leave. I didn't know what to do. My car was part of the crime scene. I had to leave it.

I started walking. I wasn't sure what to do or where to go. I felt hazy and adrift, cut loose from reality.

Exhibit 4.1 — The Aftermath

"YOU HAVE THE TOOLS"

I found myself walking to Ease, a yoga studio where my good friend, Beth Wolfe, taught. We had met during yoga and meditation training. I knew she was also certified to teach trauma-informed yoga, and she worked with veterans, police officers, and those with PTSD.

"It was such a short time," I told her, struggling to make sense of what happened. "It was nothing, really."

"I hear you," she acknowledged gently. "I also hear you minimizing the experience."

"This is crazy. It was nothing," I repeated, still dazed.

"Your brain knows that. Now. But your body didn't know that when it was happening. Your body knew it was in a life or death situation. And you are still processing it."

And then she said what I needed to hear, "You're a yoga teacher, you have the tools to deal with this."

She was right. I could feel myself vibrate—big emotional bubbles surging through my body. How many times had I told others that yoga and meditation could help us release our biggest repressed emotions?

I wouldn't have to pack away the fear until it came up years later. This was my chance to listen to my body. I breathed in, out, and kept breathing, cueing my body that it was okay to relax and that I was safe. In the midst of the storm, I could practice what I preached, do the work, and trust the process. In short, I sat my butt down and meditated like my life depended on it.

LISTENING TO MY ELEPHANT

Moral psychologist and researcher Jonathan Haidt in *The Happiness Hypothesis* wrote about my favorite metaphor for our divided mind.[22, 23] He describes our unconscious automatic intuitive brain as the "elephant" and our conscious reflective brain as the "rider."

Our elephant brain does not speak in words—it communicates through emotions and feelings. If you've ever trained a dog, it may help to think of that part of the brain similarly. We "train" our inner animal with encouragement, associating what we want—a long-term good behavior—with a good feeling. For example, for my pup, Remy, I've trained him to submit to a bath by giving him lots and lots of treats, love, and praise.

We want to train our elephant to be in sync with our rider. To do that, it helps if our unconscious elephant feels like doing what our conscious rider wants. To expedite that process, we have to get cozy with our feelings.

In the midst of my own personal storm, when what I really wanted was to be anywhere else, anyone else, I surrendered.

I sat down and listened and sat with my emotions, the fears and anxiety.

To my surprise, doing nothing and being gentle with myself was exactly what I needed.

---

22 Jonathan Haidt, The Happiness Hypothesis (New York: Basic Books, 2006).

23 I like it better than System 1 and 2, used by Kahneman in Thinking Fast and Slow. I like the terms automatic and reflective brain, used by Thaler and Sunstein in Nudge. The book Search Inside Yourself, offers a horse and rider metaphor, but like Haidt, I believe elephant is a better analogy. As a comic book nerd, I would really love it if there was a concensus to use "Hulk and Banner brain," but recognize that is wishful thinking.

It made me feel healthy and whole. In fact, it made me feel tougher, stronger, and more resilient than any other training or workout I had ever done before.

In my moment of crisis, I could *feel* the value of listening and trusting my unconscious intuition, i.e. my "elephant." In those moments of contemplation, I connected with my unconscious elephant using the "language" of care and emotion. In that space, I "told" her that I believed in her, I trusted her, I had her back, and that I would protect her just like she protected me.

It may sound totally unhinged, but oddly enough I actually felt like I was starting to become sane.

CHAPTER FIVE

EMOTIONS. WHAT'S THE POINT?

———

Perhaps the idea that people should listen to their emotions seems obvious. You wonder why I would think or feel differently. Good for you. I wish more people were like that.

My people, let's call them "the American semi-stoic working class," don't really believe in "emotions." I come from the kind of folks who make fun of entitled, Lululemon, hippy, Zen elitist spiritual gangstas. Anything too woo-woo—and that includes emotional intelligence—does not come easily to us. It certainly didn't come easily to me.

IT'S NOT IN OUR HEADS

Not long after the shooting, I was at a barbeque with my family, which included my cousin, who's a cop. I told him about what happened. He responded in his typical gruff fashion.

"Yeah, we deal with that stuff all the time, it's not a big deal," he said with a shrug as he piled on the baked beans.

In other words, it wasn't that bad. Push it down, move on, rub some dirt on it, and don't be a baby. Basically, beat my elephant mind into submission, like a grown a** adult. Naturally, I bit my lip and changed the subject. I sure as heck didn't tell him about cuddling up and communing with my intuitive spirit elephant.

Our default assumptions, beliefs, and instincts do not come out of thin air.

We are taught both implicitly and explicitly by our family and peers to be tough, gritty, and to figure it out. But the solution doesn't have to be "either-or."

We can be both tough and gentle. Sometimes we need to be soft, emotional, and even woo-woo.

This process begins with us as individuals. We can go through life fighting our elephant or we can figure out how to ride her. When our conscious and unconscious are in sync, we can use our full body wisdom and trust that our unconscious elephant isn't going to sabotage our long-term goals.

This is consistent with what I know from corporate change management consulting,

PEOPLE CHANGE WHEN THEY *FEEL* LIKE IT

I've consulted on a number of change projects for both clients and companies. Change management has evolved considerably over the last twenty years to incorporate human-centered design and storytelling. As consultants, we often puff ourselves up and make the work seem harder than it really is.

Change is simple.

People change when they *feel* like it. I use the word "feel" intentionally. Change that aligns our thoughts with our needs and desires creates a physical spark and the impulse to act. That is the kind of change that sticks.

Understanding, aligning, and working with our elephant brain can help us find our truth.

TRUSTING OUR GUT

"We human beings have lost confidence in the body just know-ing what to do."

—*HOW TO RELAX (MINDFULNESS ESSENTIALS)*
BY THICH NHAT HANH[24]

Consulting with leaders on the topics of empathy and EQ, I hear a lot of jokes about feelings. Not only am I a woman, I'm American and working class—a perfect target for my British clients to take the piss out of. That's fine, I'm happy to

---

24   Thich Nhat Hanh, How to Relax (Parallax Press, 2015).

quip back that emotional repression is probably all England's fault anyway.

For too long, we've taught men that suppressing feelings is the same as regulation. On the other end of the spectrum, we tell women that expressing emotions is acting hysterical and is a justifiable reason for firing them. This is better than locking women up in asylums, so hurray for progress!

EMOTIONS ARE NOT IMAGINARY

I once joked to an economics PhD candidate that it's funny that it took economists roughly two hundred years to "discover" emotions.[25]

"Based on the economists I know, I guess that's not too surprising." I said, with a grin.

"I don't think that is true," my friend deadpanned.

"Really?" I asked, biting hard.

"Whether or not emotions are real is still widely debated," he said, for the win.

Joking aside, when making decisions it is often useful to practice dispassion. Thaler and Sunstein, in their book *Nudge*, often use the phrase "think like an econ," differentiating

---

25 From Adam Smith in 1776 to the emergence of behavioral economics around 1976.

between the "normal" way most of us think and economical, less emotional modes of thought.

It's well understood that emotions and feelings impact our decision-making. It's the reason we are taught to avoid going to the grocery store when we're hungry or we might find our shopping cart full of sour gummy bears and nachos.

It's why we turn over our car keys before we start drinking, before our decision-making is impaired. It's also why we learn not to send emails when we're angry, realizing that we often regret what we say in moments of anger.

There is, however, a notable difference between holding space for our emotions, letting them pass through us, and ignoring or repressing them. The first is a mental and physical practice involving intentional processing and managing where we place our attention, and the second is a mindless coping mechanism.

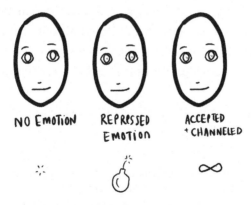

Exhibit 5.1 — We are coached to moderate the *appearance* of our emotions. What we are less practiced at is regulating and processing the emotions themselves.

EMOTIONS ARE DATA

"For a long time, emotions were viewed as noise, a nuisance, something to be ignored. But one thing we now know after more than a quarter-century of research is that emotions are not noise—rather, they are data. They reveal not just how people feel, but also what they think and how they will behave."

—SIGAL BARSADE[26]

Our unconscious elephant brain is a rapid intuitive prediction engine. If we thought through every single decision, we'd be exhausted by the cognitive load. It's estimated that about 40 percent of our day is on autopilot, although it can be much higher.[27]

We off-load and automate the boring stuff like the details of brushing our teeth, doing routine chores, and driving to work. How many times do we stop and wonder, did I really feed the dog, turn off the stove, or take out the trash?

Our elephant is also processing cues and information about people and situations, what's safe to be around, and who do we trust. This is based on unconscious pattern recognition, organic mental algorithms that includes various inputs.

Basically, many of our decisions come down to intuitive guesses and how we feel and not what we know.

---

26 Frieda Klotz, and Sigal Barsade. "Employee Emotions Aren't Noise—They're Data." MIT Sloan Management Review, 2019.

27 For more information on how much of our lives is spent on autopilot, I encourage you to check out The Power of Habit by Charles Duhig, Switch by Dan and Chip Heath, and Atomic Habits by James Clear.

WHAT YOU WANT, WHAT YOU REALLY, REALLY WANT

There is a scene in the movie *The Notebook* that illustrates how hard it can be to communicate what we want deep down.[28]

Midway through the movie, Ryan Gosling yells at Rachel McAdams, "What do you want?" Not what does her mom want, or her fiancé want, or even what he wants, but what does *she* want? He's trying to force her to find clarity.

Her face is streaked with tears, and despite her passionate undying love for him, she can't answer and she drives off, torn between her true love and her promise to her fiancé. She is also torn between financial certainty, status, her parents' approval, and the uncertainty of her heart's desire. [29]

Many of us struggle to get clear on what we want, much less to admit it. This is partly because our mind, heart, and body are often at odds. We weren't trained to listen to those signals. We are social creatures and we don't always know how to tell the difference between our own desires and other people's.

Making new and novel decisions takes energy. It is easier to default to habit or defer to social norms or let others tell us what we should do. Staying within our tribe feels safe, not least of all because many of us were trained from an early age not to speak up, not to take up space, not to be needy, and not to be difficult.

---

28 I realize that Nicholas Sparks may not seem like the most academic reference. However, I find movies, especially popular ones, are great ways to analyze emotions and social norms.

29 If you prefer a similar conflict with a different outcome, consider the ending of Casablanca, where the heroine chooses duty over Humphrey Bogart and love.

SOCIAL NORMS ARE HAND-ME-DOWN DECISIONS

When we unpack social norms and manners, we start to realize they are just communal habits, old algorithmic rules, based on decisions made by previous generations. These norms are not updated with our preferences or even with current data. They are, in essence, simply the decisions that kept the tribe safe in the past.

If we don't pause to ask what we want, then how can we really please anyone?

It's like wearing an ugly dress passed down for generations, only to learn that it never really fit our great, great, great, great, great grand-whoever, and she only picked the color because she thought her husband's favorite color was pink, but it turned out he was color-blind and was just saying what he thought she wanted to hear.

Basically, it's like a freakin' O'Henry story.

To unlearn all this, we have to question assumptions. We have to become aware of how decisions are made and why they are not. That is one of the purposes of meditation and surrounding ourselves with mentors who can help broaden our understanding.

This is the process of opening up to both our energetic flow and the energetic needs that surround us.

CHAPTER SIX

THE SHAPE OF EMOTIONS

———

Most of my life, I've chased flow in one form or another.

For over twenty years, I played competitive ultimate frisbee all over the United States and world, which allowed me to find sublime moments of connection with my teammates on the field and off.

I also found flow when solving complex problems for Fortune 500 companies. I found it diving into data, blending data sets, and creating stories from insights. I found it in art, in writing, and even in my feeble attempts at poetry. I found it waiting for me in Savasana, the final resting pose of my yoga practice as my consciousness floated into the universe.

I reveled in flow—until I lost it.

I found myself stuck in a culture where I just couldn't make it work, where I wasn't wanted or needed. I felt lost. My fire gutted out and my heart broke.

LOSING MY FLOW FELT LIKE LOSING MYSELF.
That experience forced me to step back.

Ha.

I write that as if I had a choice. It was more like I'd been run off the road. I crashed so hard I was an unrecognizable puddle.

I'd always been able to get through any challenge by pouring on the gas. I had assumed I had endless reserves of enthusiasm. Looking back, I realize I was just really good at finding my flow.

Flow by definition is generative, meaning that it creates energy. I'd always felt that work, even work other people described as difficult or tedious, was easy and even fun.

I loved work. Until I found myself in a situation where I didn't. As I felt flow slipping further and further away, pouring on the gas only made things worse.

I didn't know it at the time, but I was burning out.

FLOW AND BURNOUT
I was burnt out in a way that is increasingly common to post-digital generations, to those caught in increasingly truncated cycles of innovation and transformation—a form of burnout that is at once unique and increasingly ubiquitous.

My intuitive ability to find flow, as well as my experience of burnout, drove me to get really clear on what creates and destroys energy, motivation, and drive. It led me to dig into the research and myself.

My thesis is simple: if flow is the essence of what it means to be our best most creative human self, burnout is what occurs when we experience dehumanization, directly and indirectly, when we work in systems and organizations that dismiss emotions and expect us to function like automatons.

GETTING CURIOUS AND LISTENING MORE.
So, for over a year I interviewed people and my clients. I asked them to not just talk about their feelings. I wanted to know what happiness and confidence looked and felt like for them. I made them analyze and diagram their emotion, in surveys and on napkins. I wanted to understand what was beneath their surface.

I used Csikszentmihalyi's match quality graph, in part because I wondered how much time in boredom doing scut work other people tolerated. As I had conversations, things got interesting.

I spoke to men, women, folks in transition, young and old, across sectors and industries—basically anyone who would talk to me about emotions and feelings. I even made my dad, who does not talk about feelings, talk about why he doesn't talk about feelings. I learned a lot along the way, including that our emotional literacy is pretty limited.

Okay, here is where things are going to get weird.

I learned that the way we actually feel and the way we want to feel often varies. I assumed everyone would want to be in the flow and challenged all the time. I assumed everyone had the same emotional intuition.

My assumptions were wrong.

SUPPORTING EMPLOYEE NEEDS

I'm impressed by proactive companies like Google that use data to intentionally change and modify incentive systems and acknowledge the need for emotional safety. In his book *Work Rules!*, Google's former head of people Laszlo Bock describes how managers' responsibilities and incentives were shifted to focus on coaching their team while removing their responsibility to judge, assess, hire, and promote.[30] In addition, Google empowers individual employees to "vote with their feet" and change teams when they feel like they don't "fit."

I was curious. How do empowered people and folks who describe themselves as relatively happy really feel about their work?

In the course of two years, I've probably had a little over a hundred conversations asking people to track and graph their emotions.

This was not particularly scientific at all and quantitative data geeks will find my methodology messy. This is by nature a

---

30 Laszlo Bock, Work Rules! (New York: Hachette Book Group, 2015).

qualitative and squishy exercise that was initially really only meant for me.

Most folks I spoke with had to "warm up" to the idea of listening to their emotions. This was not easy or intuitive, so I allowed folks a great deal of latitude in answering. Some folks mapped their emotions retrospectively looking at their calendars for the week, while some choose to do it in real time.

A FEW THOUGHTS ABOUT "MEASURING" EMOTIONS

"You and I are both strangely comfortable talking about emotions in a way that most people just aren't," my friend and mentor Anjana Sreedar said to me one summer evening on a rooftop overlooking Manhattan.

We were discussing a recent disappointing collaboration experience. A start-up team I'd been working on had fallen apart, and I was sad and frustrated. I had learned the hard way that even "nice" people and those trained in EQ and empathy can still get triggered and act in an exclusionary way.

Make no mistake; raw emotional honesty is often uncomfortable, even for professionals. It's risky sharing how we feel, and we are well advised to proceed with caution. We don't need to share everything. In fact, sometimes just sharing that we don't feel like sharing is a good start.

Some tips for sharing our feelings.

- **Make sure you are in a good place**—stress and discomfort, either physical or emotional, can make us myopic or competitive.

- **Move softly**—use your emotions to "wayfind." Until you get the hang of it and gel with your team, slow down, listen more, and notice your emotional and somatic (body) responses to what is being said.

- **Always Maintain the "container"**—This advice comes from the book *Crucial Conversations,* which is a fantastically useful read.[31] Establishing trust and respect are necessary for productive collaborations. When trust and respect is missing or lost, we can either step away until they can be reestablished or accept that we are in a transactional/competitive environment.

- **Start with the question**—How can we build trust moving forward? What can I do to reassure you, which elements of flow are we missing (clarity, feedback, control, and so on)? What do you need to focus on the team goal?

THE SKILLS CHALLENGES—CONNECTING WITH EMOTION

I wasn't the first to connect emotions with the research of flow. Csikszentmihalyi made the connection between the experience of flow and emotions in his research. I first saw this chart while working in an unsupportive workplace feeling underemployed and bored. At the time, I was desperate

---

31   Kerry Patterson, Joseph Grenny, Ron McMilan, Al Switzler, Crucial Conversations, (New York: McGraw Hill, 2009).

to understand appropriate boundaries and how much boring work anyone should have to endure. His chart was an important piece of that puzzle.

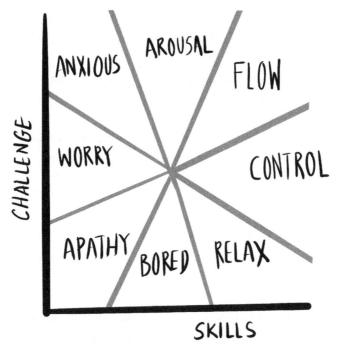

Exhibit 6.1 — The Skills Challenge Graph or Match Quality graph based on the work of Mihaly Csikszentmihalyi, PhD.

After talking to many people, I found that some folks have a hard time differentiating between all eight emotions. As I dug into the research on emotional intelligence, I'd learn my finding was not uncommon. According to social researcher Brené Brown, some people can only identify three emotions, specifically mad, sad, and glad.[32] So for folks who preferred it, I consolidated the eight emotions in the chart above, into four categories.

- Excited—includes "arousal" and some flow.[33]

- Controlled—includes controlled flow and feeling relaxed.

- Stress—includes feeling worried, frustrated, anxious, and generally over stimulated.

- Bored—includes apathetic, under stimulated, low energy, low challenge, low importance, and low meaning.

DE GUSTIBUS
"My worries make me work harder."

—MELINDA GATES[34]

After talking to many people, I discovered that how people felt and how they wanted to feel varied a great deal. We all have different appetites for risk and different experiences, which means what brings us to our unknown edge and creates anxiety or fear is different for each of us. The wisest and more experienced people embraced those challenges.

---

32 Brené Brown, (host), "Dr. Marc Brackett and Brené on 'Permission to Feel,'" Unlocking Us, April 14, 2020.

33 I discovered the word "arousal" makes even grown-ups giggle.

34 love this quote by Melinda Gates, who, if I had to guess, I'd say is a Minerva type. Melinda Gates, The Moment of Lift How Empowering Women Changes the World (New York: Flat Iron Books 2019).

For the majority of people, the upper right-hand side—toward flow—was generally considered "positive."

Even given that, I'd prefer not to ascribe a valence—making the assessment that an emotion is positive or negative, good or bad is a judgment call and it varies. For example, more than a few folks have said some variation of the phrase, "some stress is good." Others have said that there are times when they liked getting boring, repetitive, easily automatable work where they could just phone it in. Like Einstein working as a patent clerk, there are times when low challenge work is just what we want.

The valence, whether something was good or bad, depended on perspective, life stage, and the gap between expectations and reality.

Two things I found held true. First, most people generally want some flow, and second, to get there it helps to have a modicum of emotional safety.

HEALTHY SHAPES
I did find that certain patterns repeat among folks who said they were relatively happy.

So, I made personas around these generalities.

They are the Spartan, Firecracker, Guru, Minerva, and Gardener.

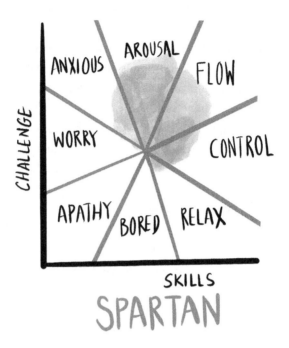

These are folks with a medium to high-risk appetite. They are the folks who take big swings. Many have had past successes and are often considered a proven commodity. Generally, these are what most folks in America identify as high-confidence individuals. Nearly all the comments that said "some stress is good" came from this group.

This group skewed male but was not exclusively male. Many women, returning to work and/or gearing up for a new challenge as their kids grew up, also identified as part of this group.

Spartans expect and demand challenges. They have a tendency to either be unaware of risks or to push through, confident that if they bite off more than they can chew, they will either be able to hustle or find leverage or resources to close the gap. This group can be risk seeking and is prone to imposter syndrome. If they feel unsupported, they may cover up their insecurities by putting others down.

Earn their trust and reward them for being honest and vulnerable about their concerns.

FIRECRACKER SHAPE

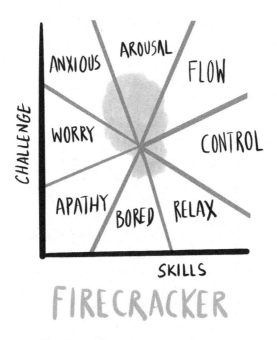

These are generally high-potential rookies. This group has a lot of confidence, possibly due to the Dunning Kruger effect, and they don't always know what they don't know. They have a lot of energy that needs to be channeled and make excellent workhorses. Like Spartans. they also are prone to imposter syndrome. They are often part of the team that the Spartan leverages. Generally, they have a high-value technical skill that they are eager to grow and develop. Often, unless there is some other setback, the Firecracker grows into a Spartan.

They have a tendency to avoid or off-load work that they consider "boring," administrative, or low value, unless there is something in it for them like recognition, compensation, or some other external reward. This group skews younger.

Both Firecrackers and Spartans report that they do well in hierarchical competitive cultures.

THE GURU SHAPE

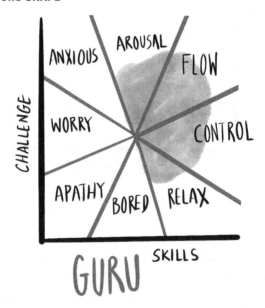

This group skewed older and included several retirees. This group has earned the right to do what it wants. It also included the folks who felt like they were at the top of their game, those who had figured out how to balance their work/life portfolio. Notably, they had both the autonomy and resources to intentionally create their own work portfolio. They also had the ability to walk away and fire clients.

This group tends to be very self-aware, intentional, and psychologically mature, and they are often the leaders of an organization. More often than not, they both reflect and create the cultures that they are in. Most of these folks were also in long-term, stable, and self-described "healthy" relationships.

MINERVA SHAPE

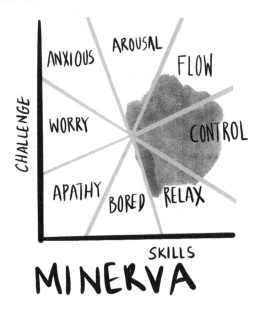

This shape is named for both Professor McGonagall and the Roman goddess of war and wisdom. On the other side of flow from The Spartan, this is the overachieving, focused high performer that may be a bit of a perfectionist. Minervas have super high standards. They aren't necessarily the ones screaming as they charge into battle, they just quietly unsheathe their sword and get to work. They don't need much "fanfare"—many even hate the spotlight and public recognition. They are most motivated by the joy of doing the work and, when applicable, a purpose either aligned with the organization or perhaps their family's success.

Like Spartans, their impact increases with leverage and power. Unlike Spartans, they are more deliberate about the risks they take.

Whereas Spartans have learned that they can leap before they look, Minervas don't write checks their butts can't cash. In part, this is because they are the ones with the deepest skill sets, which makes them the ones most often called upon to back up Spartans and Firecrackers who overreach.

We destroy a Minerva's trust by expecting him to act like a Spartan, not trusting his risk assessment, or expecting him to act in performative ways that feel insincere. Give a Minerva a direction and let him do his thing.

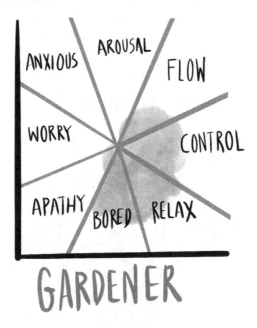

This group is often content to play the long game, planting seeds and tending the garden for the long term. This group appreciates playing their role. They don't need, or want, stress and they may be happy to do the algorithmic work. As Gardeners evolve, they may take on more authority emerging to become a Minerva or Guru, or they may be content playing a support role. Leaders should continue to check in with them about their needs and may need to nudge them away from complacency and boredom. At the very least, regular check-ins signal that leadership is not taking them for granted.

They may not ask for as many rewards as Firecrackers, but smart organizations should be careful not to overlook or take their dependability for granted.

UNHEALTHY SHAPES AND BURNOUT

As we can see, healthy shapes are mostly "above the diagonal fold"—in the upper right quadrant between skills and challenges.

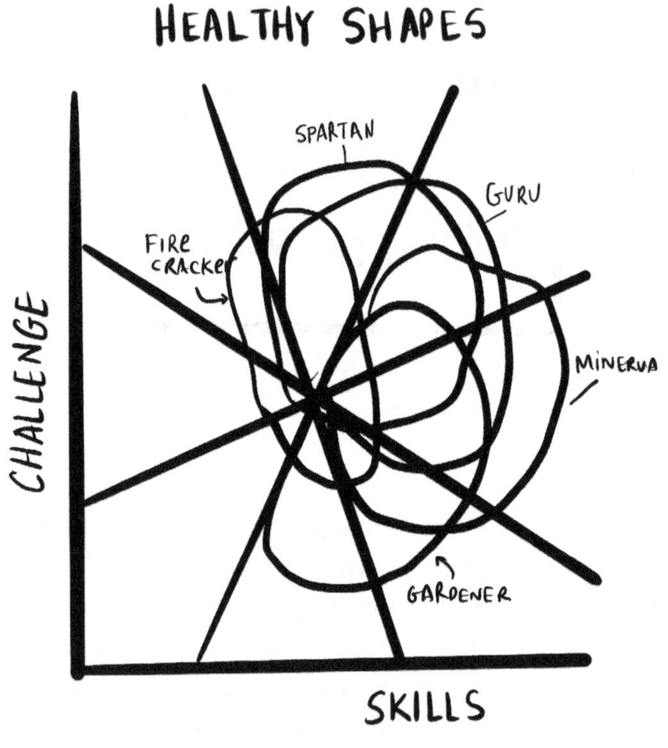

Exhibit 6.2 – Graph of all the healthy shapes together

"Below the fold," things get messy.

Some folks waste a lot of energy "bouncing" between stress, boredom, and apathy. People in stress or anxiety feel triggered and over stimulated. Interestingly, some folks also said feeling bored triggered an impulse to avoid boredom, making them even more anxious and stressed.

Some folks reported relaxing when they felt they hadn't earned it, which made them feel anxious.

Lack of control of activities or time, whether real or imagined, is a huge source of stress that can send some folks into a tailspin. Feeling helpless keeps folks on high alert and results in an inability to relax and recharge. It also results in folks wasting effort, trying to control things outside of their control, or being unable to relax enough to get into the groove.

WHY UNDERSTANDING THIS MAY HELP

First, it helps to know that the most successful people structure their activity portfolio in a way that makes them happy. I hope this opens up the conversation about who is entitled to opportunities and flow.

I also hope it helps folks shift from feeling the dissonance of different preferences to learning how complementary styles work together and can align.

Inexperienced managers manage people based on their own default assumptions. This is not an accusation; most of us do this until we figure out a better way. For example, if we are a Spartan, we may assume others feel like we do. We tend to encourage and motivate folks according to what worked for us.

Consider the common advice "fake it 'til you make it," which works well for many Spartans and Firecrackers. Many folks resist this particular piece of advice in part because it feels inauthentic and risky. Personally, it makes my skin crawl.

Noted psychology professor and biofeedback researcher Amy Cuddy suggests reframing that advice as "fake it until you become it."[35] I like what my friend and consultant Neelay Bhatt called it in his 2017 DC Startup Week talk.

"PRACTICE"

Yup, good old-fashioned practice. He used the example of his 2014 TED Talk, to show new entrepreneurs what we can do to get good at anything. Basically, it comes down to lots and lots of practice. This is especially important when working with Gardeners and Minervas who may be more risk averse than Firecrackers and Spartans. We can help them build the confidence to step up their game by providing the opportunity and feedback to prepare and to perfect their craft.

When coaching folks to push through their fears and uncertainties, we have to make sure we understand what they are seeing and feeling. They may notice things that we don't, things that are instinctively obvious to them and assume that we are ignoring or doubting their instinct. If we are not aware of this dynamic, we may be communicating that we don't care about or respect their intuition, or that we don't care about what they need to feel confident.

---

35 Amy Cuddy often talks about "fake it until you become it" in both her 2012 TED Talk and also her book *Presence*.

USING OUR EMOTIONS TO WAYFIND

In Part Three, we'll go a bit deeper into how to run experiments to change our emotional shape—shifting the way we look at things, what we do, and even how to get what we want from others.

Once we are clear about how we feel, it may help to revisit the Flow List. When I reflect on the nine characteristics of flow, it often "sparks" an idea to help me get unstuck.

A FEW THINGS I LEARNED AFTER A HUNDRED CONVERSATIONS

Before diving into the Flow List, I wanted to share some thoughts about navigating these shapes.

MANAGING OVERACHIEVERS

Overachievers often feel anxious when they are bored or have nothing to do. They get stressed because they are bored and don't know how to relax. Ping-ponging between these negative states can leave them feeling untethered or at loose ends. If this goes on for too long, they risk burnout, and organizations risk losing their talent. Reward them for practicing and modeling good mindful habits like resting, giving positive feedback, and taking vacations.

HIGH STATUS HIGH PERFORMERS APPEAR TO BE GRASPING

One relatively young police officer I interviewed pointed to the high challenge, low skill quadrant on Csikszentmihalyi's chart and told me definitively, "That is where I want to be, all day every day."

"Are you sure?" I asked.

"Without a doubt," he nodded.

High risk, high reward—that is where people maximize growth. Even when I pointed out that the emotions associated with that area were worry, stress, and anxiety, he insisted that was where he wanted to be. What took me aback was that he was so certain he was entitled to work in a role that far exceeded his skills, even after I pointed this out.

Based on my limited survey, high performers, especially Spartans and Firecrackers, don't always think a lot about managing emotions. Higher status individuals assume that they'll only tolerate so much bullsh*t. They are unapologetic for pushing for opportunities. High status, high performers have clear limits and expectations, which they expect to be maintained.

I'll admit that this triggered my own frustrations, especially when I felt that they came from someone who I felt was not entitled to them. I had to check my own judgment. I wasn't angry at other people's boundaries; I was angry that my own boundaries weren't always respected.

It didn't feel fair and this feeling triggered a lot of uncomfortable emotions.

All people have status and power. Some of it earned and some of it assumed. I was reminded power is only partially correlated with competence, talent, and ability. Status comes from many sources, including unearned privileges like inherited wealth and being born in the right century.

THE SECOND ACT

Interestingly, I found that when some women hit their midlife, they became more assertive. Several women told me they quit the corporate world when they either "couldn't play the game anymore" or when they were blocked from opportunities they'd been promised.

One graphic artist told me, "It was less risky to start my business as a freelancer than to work for people who did not see my value." As Patty McCord, former head of people at Netflix, said in her TED Talk, to be paid what they are worth, women need to walk.[36] However, walking away from one's investment in a company may also be a risk.

What would happen if companies tapped into their employees' full potential, if women didn't have to quit in order to access growth opportunities, if instead companies allowed women and really all marginalized folks to reach their full potential?

WE CAN'T AFFORD TO BE OBLIVIOUS

We can no longer afford to ignore our deep feelings of this fundamental unfairness. Being oblivious to our teammates' suffering is inhumane and dehumanizing, not to mention just crappy.

Some leaders, when confronted with the harm they have unconsciously created, automatically respond:

---

36 Patty McCord, "HR lessons from the world of Silicon Valley start-ups," TED, June 2015.

They should have said something.

Why didn't they speak up sooner?

I had no idea people felt this way.

I get it. Frankly, guilt and shame are energy blockers and are not useful for building collaboration. It's embarrassing for leaders when we mess up and realize we've been inconsiderate knuckleheads. We've all been there.

The sooner we admit our mistake and apologize, the quicker we can work to reestablish trust and create a solution that benefits everyone.

We have to stop putting the onus for change on folks with the least power. It is the leader's job to check in and ask. It is the leader's job to lead, to set the tone. It is the leader's job to create a space where people can trust and communicate their perspective including their intuitions and feelings.

I understand that it's easier to stick our heads in the sand and pretend emotions don't exist and avoid tough conversations.

Dealing with emotions is hard.

It's a good thing we're capable of doing hard things.

II

THE FLOW LIST

CHAPTER SEVEN

THE FLOW LIST

—

"The adrenaline, the rush... I call it the hum. There's a hum that happens inside my head when I hit a certain writing rhythm, a certain speed. When laying track goes from feeling like climbing a mountain on my hands and knees to feeling like flying effortlessly through the air... Everything inside me just shifts."

— SHONDA RHIMES[37]

We've talked a lot about how flow is the feeling of being our best and brightest selves. It was the experience of losing flow and burning out that set me on this journey. Returning to my energetic center helped me uncover the language to clarify unconscious assumptions and communicate what we all need to do our best work.

"YOU LACK CONFIDENCE."

My corporate career started to crumble when I was assigned to work for a "devil wears Brooks Brothers" kind of partner,

---

37 Shonda Rhymes, Year of Yes (New York: Simon & Schuster, 2015).

the kind who expected deference and unquestioning loyalty. Slowly at first and then more quickly, I saw the tight-knit collaboration I'd once enjoyed began to dissolve. Working remotely, I was initially unaware of the impact this had on my work.

After this partner took over, he decreed that I "lacked confidence." Soon after that, his lieutenants and minions started to echo this criticism.

Over the next period of time, despite hustling (mostly on low-value internal projects), I failed to move the needle. I could feel my spark fading and with it my self-worth. At the time, I believed the feedback was offered in good faith and responded by bearing down, determined to earn my new team's trust.

In retrospect, I needn't have bothered. When I finally left, one director dismissively commented, "What did you expect? You're competing against people who can code in their sleep." My stomach dropped as I realized I'd wasted my time focusing on the wrong problem. It was never about my confidence.

I may be proficient in many areas, but I'm not a coder. I'm an analyst, a strategist, a designer, and storyteller, among other things. My "coding skills," such as they were, were just the scraps I'd picked up PM-ing technical projects—tricks that I needed to unravel short-term problems. I was baffled. I thought they knew this, or should have. After all, I'd helped build and update the team's skills inventory. The data was there. They just had to care enough to look.

I've never felt more invisible in my life.

Months later, another consultant reminded me that what I experienced was quite common, especially for women and especially when there is a change in leadership. She reminded me there is a reason consulting is called "burn and churn."[38]

When I eventually left, I felt ashamed, confused, and bullied. I didn't realize just how dehumanizing and emotionally exhausting that experience was. It wasn't until after I came across a checklist for burnout, including lethargy, cynicism, and emotional exhaustion, in the book *No Hard Feelings* that I had a name for my experience.[39]

When I opened up about my experience and told the people who knew me how I was blamed for my lack of confidence, their response was generally some combination of outrage and WTF. Most folks describe me as pretty normal although they admit I can be kind of intense, occasionally fierce, and even a little bit scary.

Being told I was "lacking confidence" was bizarre. Some suggested it was intended to distract and demotivate me. I don't know if that was the intention, although that is certainly how it felt at the time. The research suggests that their intentions were not so nefarious. The team, alerted by the partner's opinion, was simply collecting evidence to support his point of view.

---

38 Fwiw, I do not believe that management consulting must be cutthroat and dehumanizing. Prior to this experience, I'd spent seven mostly positive years on many cross-functional teams. I had a lot of respect for my co-workers and leaders. However, in an organization of over one hundred thousand people, cultures fragment. In a results-oriented company, without careful oversight, values sometimes take a back seat to money and status.

39 Liz Fosslien and Mollie West Duffy, No Hard Feelings: The Secret Power of Embracing Emotions At Work (New York: Portfolio/Penguin, 2019).

Knowing all this, I would have acted differently. I certainly wouldn't have taken such feedback to heart. However, at the time, I'd invested a great deal of energy helping to starting up the innovation group and was eager to see it through.

Yes, I knew about sunk costs.

But there is a difference in knowing the path and walking the path. I'd be damned if I was going to give up, which is how I discovered that there is such a thing as being *too* tenacious.

GRIT GONE WILD

"When I started at The Office, I had zero confidence. Whenever Greg Daniels came into the room to talk to our small group of writers, I was so nervous that I would raise and lower my chair involuntarily, like a tic. Finally, weeks in, writer Mike Schur put his hand on my arm and said, gently, "You have to stop." Years later I realized that the way I had felt during those first few months was correct. I didn't deserve to be confident yet. I happen to believe that no one inherently deserves anything, except basic human rights, and not to have to watch an ad before you watch a trailer on YouTube."

—MINDY KALING[40]

In my deep dive into the topic of confidence, I found Mindy Kaling's quote very appealing. Grit and tenacity are both accessible and controllable. My work ethic had always helped

---

40 Mindy Kaling, Why Not Me? (New York: Crown Archetype, 2015).

me find flow. As discussed previously, grit is part of the process for finding flow.

Unfortunately, grit isn't always enough.

I wasn't igniting. Instead, I was grinding down, stuck in a rut, spinning my wheels and running out of gas, if not metaphors.

Flow and power create confidence and a sense of worthiness. The opportunity to practice doing work that has meaning is what truly builds confidence. Unfortunately, those opportunities are also correlated with the perception of status and power and depend on how well we "play the game."

DIGGING INTO THE RESEARCH ON CONFIDENCE

I could mention how feedback about soft skills is often specious feedback given to low status individuals. I could mention how over 90 percent of women have been told in written reviews that they lack confidence compared to 5 percent of men. That mindless personality-based feedback is not only unhelpful, but it's destructive, unclear and unkind.

No one can prove himself or herself when their worth has already been determined in advance.

THE GOLDEN RULE WORKS BOTH WAYS

Confidence is a feeling, an intuitive gut calculation.

I wish I had stepped back and held my former bosses accountable for the sheer hubris required to dictate to me how I felt.

Hadn't I facilitated and led dozens of design sprints? Hadn't I coached dozens of teams and clients on the value of empathy and active listening? How was I expected to give grace, empathy, trust, and respect without expecting any in return?

These questions are rhetorical. The problem was that my default setting, after working with a collaborative team, was still stuck on giver or "sucker" mode.

F**K PROVING YOURSELF (TO A POINT)

Looking back at the Flow List, characteristics that define flow were things that were no longer automatically given to me by my colleagues.

The Flow List were the principles that "bright and shiny" new hires and those with status were given without question. All my grittiness and experience had proved was that I was a chump. I wasn't worthy of feedback, clarity, work that fit my skills, autonomy, or respect, much less trust.

I have to admit, I'd seen this play out before when other folks had been pushed out. Treat someone like crap, bully them into quitting, and if that doesn't work, set them up to fail. When we see people as simply replaceable cogs or competition, it's easy to rationalize disposing of them when we want an upgrade.

It wasn't personal for them. To them, people were cogs and replaceable. I was just completely unprepared for that kind of leadership.

THE NINE PRINCIPLES OF FLOW WORK

When we are part of the in-group, on a healthy team, we take these principles for granted and they seem pretty fundamental and basic.

I learned the hard way what happens when we don't clarify the baseline fundamental expectations, of what it means to work with dignity and respect. Bullies can take advantage of cooperators and the results are cultures that destroy diversity, trust, dignity, and respect.

My hope is that everyone can use this list to assess work situations that are even a little bit "off." The first eight characteristics of flow are from Csikszentmihalyi's book and TED Talk with the addition of "Love and Care."

In summary they are:

- **Match Quality**—Our skills and challenges are aligned, and we are in the sweet spot of growth.
- **Clarity**—We know what action comes next and ideally the "north star" goal.
- **Feedback**—We know what is working and what is not. We know how we can improve and iterate, or at least we can get the feedback we need when we need it.
- **Control**—We feel like we have the right level of control and autonomy over our decisions for the task. When we make a suggestion, it is acknowledged and evaluated appropriately.
- **Focus**—We experience an energetic and intense focus. Our team and manager understand and support our priorities.

- **Everyday Life Falls Away**—The daily cares and the mundane world falls away. Our team and manager understand and respect our boundaries.
- **Selfless**—There is a sense of nonbeing and a loss of ego, and we feel a purpose and higher reason. There are people on the team that have our back and vice versa.
- **Timeless**—Our sense of time expands and shifts. We can also control and manipulate our schedule to support our work.
- **Love and Care**—Finally, we feel a sense of care, perhaps even energetic love, for our work, our team, or community.

FLOW IS NONNEGOTIABLE...

The Flow List is a baseline for creating human and dignified working environments.

As employees, we expect our work will be relatively safe physically and we'll be paid on time; however, some folks believe all we can and should expect from an employer ends at legal obligations and OSHA compliance.

Perhaps the belief that flow is a human right is quixotic. I've been accused of being naive. Personally, I think the folks who call me naive are shortsighted. I'll also point out that the leaders that have called me naive to my face also assume *they* deserve the right to be respected and trusted.

Social media and increased transparency around the employee experience show us that dignity is a real possibility.

While the list is nonnegotiable, in general, the specific terms for each principle are fluid. Everything is a balance and contextual. For example, Sheryl Sandberg has been dragged hard on social media by some groups, especially with women of color, for her advice to "lean in."

That advice worked for her, and I suspect for many folks like her in the tech world, but it clearly doesn't work for all groups in all situations; it doesn't work for the folks in the out-group or who are assumed to be leverage.[41]

One thing I've found reading over two hundred business books in two years is that most advice works for some people, some of the time. What we need depends on whether we are in a safe cooperative team environment or a competitive environment. It depends on the objectives, where we are on the spectrum, and it depends on how good we are at negotiating for what we need. So sometimes the answer is indeed to lean in and sometimes, we need to listen to some Fat Joe and consider leaning back.

USE THE FLOW LIST MEDITATIONS TO FEEL BETTER

For each of the Flow List principles, I've included some stories and meditations that may be useful. My goal is to plant a seed to inspire a shift to move away from less desired feelings like worry, apathy, or boredom and up and to the right into more desired emotional states like flow, control and excitement.

Entire books could be and have been written on each of these topics. Part Two provides a starter list to help us begin notice these principles in our everyday lives.

---

41   Claire Suddath, and Rebecca Greenfield, "After Five Years of Leaning in, Everything and Nothing Has Changed," Bloomberg.Com, 2018.

CHAPTER EIGHT

MATCH QUALITY

—

In the Shape of Emotion, we discussed the chart below, which illustrates the relationship between flow and skills and challenge. The chart is one of the most referenced pieces of Csikszentmihalyi's research.

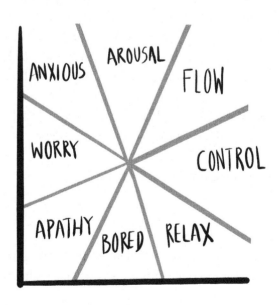

Exhibit 8.1 - Match Quality Chart.

Csikszentmihalyi uses this chart to illustrate how balancing skills and challenges lead to flow. Recently, I've discovered economists have another term, which I like better. The fit between skills, proclivities, strengths, and work, is also referred to as "match quality."

According to a 2018 Gallup survey, only 34 percent of employees consider themselves engaged at work.[42] A big part of low engagement is poor match quality. Better alignment can result in improved productivity, retention, and psychological safety. Some organizations already enable this. For example, former McKinsey consultant Safi Bahcall, in his bestselling book *Loonshots*, credits an internal incentives consultant—responsible for ensuring match quality—for saving his job.

In his first gig for the consulting giant, Bahcall was stuck working on a project that was outside both his area of expertise and interest. When it bombed, he felt certain he was going to be canned. Fortunately, McKinsey understood that bad fits happen and instead of firing him, they put him to better use.

What would the world be like if the 66 percent of folks who weren't engaged were kicking it on all cylinders?

My guess? Freakin' awesome!

INTRINSIC MOTIVATION

Match quality is an essential element in creating intrinsic motivation, the internal motivation associated with creativity,

---

42   Jim Harper, Employee Engagement on the Rise in the U.S., Gallup.com, 8/26/2018.

meaning, and purpose. This seems obvious, since by definition it includes those challenges that fit our interests, proclivities, and strengths.

As our extrinsic needs are met and we feel more secure and can afford to think longer term, we can start to care more about our higher level or intrinsic motivators. Put another way, we're less willing to put up with crap when we feel like our basic needs are assured. Unfortunately, research shows businesses suck at managing for intrinsic motivation. That's why we need to learn how to,

ASK FOR WHAT WE NEED
"I always deserve the best treatment because I never put up with any other."
—EMMA WOODHOUSE, *EMMA* BY JANE AUSTEN

People gravitate toward doing work that fits within their strengths and interests. Many of us also find work that delivers value and serves a need to be motivating. Unfortunately, some organizations and leaders often get in the way of that natural inclination.

If my study of the shape of emotions taught me anything, it was that successful people ask for what they need and get it. What was less clear was whether the relationship between the two is correlated or causal.

Regardless, we all deserve to be heard and accommodated fairly. It's that last bit, "fairly," that is hard to get right.

STUFF THAT GETS IN THE WAY OF FIT

Part of the issue, at least from my perspective as an American, is our complicated relationship with status and our American legacy of exclusion and dehumanization. In the United States, we have a belief that we are egalitarian, have a low power distance, and our systems are built on meritocracy.[43]

For people who succeed, this narrative feels true, but for others it's often chalked up to bad luck. However, if we step back and look at the data, "bad luck" looks a lot like bias.

By definition, if it's not true for everyone then it's not fair.

Therefore, we must conclude that the US is not egalitarian. We are not meritocratic; we are a country in an unconscious class cold war. It sucks, not least of all because it's inefficient and mean.

JOB CRAFTING FOR FLOW

"A growing body of research suggests that an exercise we call 'job crafting' can be a powerful tool for reenergizing and reimagining your work life. It involves redefining your job to incorporate your motives, strengths, and passions."[44]

—AMY WRZESNIEWSKI

---

43 I first learned about the Power Distance Index, like so many ideas, from one of Malcolm Gladwell's books. Gladwell is a master of blending stories and academic research in ways that are both profound, fascinating, and useful. Malcolm Gladwell, Outliers (New York: Little Brown and Company, 2008, p. 204–217).

44 Amy Wrzesniewski, *Managing Yourself: Turn the Job You Have Into the Job You Want*. [online] Harvard Business Review, 2010.

People job craft to create meaning, purpose, and to be more aligned with their strengths and needs. High status folks and those in the in-group are granted more latitude to do this. One risk of job crafting for low status folks is that the extra work may be taken for granted, undervalued, and/or underappreciated. Managers can turn a gift into an obligation and in the process create resentment in the jobcrafter.

Although job crafting is not new, the term is. It makes sense to divide group tasks based on talents and interests. For example, splitting the sales roles into hunter and gatherer aspects to optimize sales is now a common practice.

It's impossible not to see the connection between what is valued and what is rewarded, both through recognition and money. Over time, this gets baked into our system, as what is valued is linked to status.

Status, power, and control are all factors that distort match quality and fit.

Job descriptions are often created based on the previous incumbents' strengths, which may be a reflection of the high-status leadership strengths and don't necessarily reflect the organizational needs. Like an echo from the past, the hiring process is unconsciously weighted toward past needs and may be blind to new opportunities, skills, and qualities.

SCUT WORK

"If you mess this up, I will bury you in scut work." You hear this kind of threat every other episode on *Grey's Anatomy*. We may not know what "scut work" is, but we know it means less time doing the "real work" of surgery. This kind of drama makes for entertaining television, but it's a crap way to lead in real life.

The good news is one of the byproducts of the scrutinization of healthcare billing is that there is ample data explaining who provides what services and what their skills and certifications are.

Studies show that working *beneath* one's skill level is a factor leading to burnout.[45] Those studies also suggest that "low status" folks, including historically underrepresented groups, get assigned more scut work and have less access to "glamorous" work. I don't argue that everyone has to pay their dues, but it is clear that this is "truer" for some groups than others; "lower status" groups take longer on average to be promoted, despite equal and often better credentials.

SCUT, GRIND, AND BOREDOM SERVE A PURPOSE

Off-loading scut work may be counter effective. In fact, scut work can be a valuable part of the creative process. Lower value, mindless work can be restorative and even provide valuable frontline insights for uncovering new opportunities and efficiencies.

---

45 Philip A. Masters, February 5, 2019. "Practice at the Top of Your License: What Does That Really Mean?" [online] KevinMD.com.

In his book *Wherever You Go There You Are*, Jon Kabatt-Zin describes how some monks find meditation and flow in doing the dishes. I remembered this part because I didn't grow up with a dishwashing machine and can 100 percent relate. Doing the dishes by hand doesn't require intentional focus, and our mind can relax as our hands scrub, warmed by the hot water.[46]

THERE IS ALWAYS A WAY

Jennifer DiMotta, former CMO and consultant, has spent most of her career in on the cutting edge of digital marketing. With over twenty years of experience in digital marketing and e-commerce, she has had to learn to lead and grow, managing a mix of creatives, quants, and engineers in a fluid environment.[47]

When managing people, she naturally looks for the win, win, win.

"Fundamentally, I want my people to succeed, to do the best work they can, for my team and the company," she told me, in the middle of what turned out to be a three-mile hike including Arlington National Cemetery and the Washington Monument.

"What do you do when what they are good at doesn't align with what you need?" I asked, a little out of breath, having lost endurance after my third ACL surgery. DiMotta, in contrast, hasn't stopped running since her days in basic training and it showed.

---

46 Jon Kabir-Zinn, Wherever You Go, There You Are (New York: Hachette Books, 2005).

47 Jennifer DiMotta, Interview Washington, DC, March 24, 2018.

"Sometimes what they *think* they want isn't necessarily what they are good at or what we need," she said, then told me about how she recently had to reengineer someone's job to focus on one channel, rather than multiple channels. "She [the mentee] was disappointed. To her it felt like a demotion, but the move helped her focus and deepen her skills."

"I really haven't come across a situation where I wasn't able to find a solution that worked for everyone," she added. "People have peak skills, some are smart, compassionate, technical, common sense... whatever their peak is, I make the most of those, and help them understand and respect the talents of others."

Jen's approach reminds me of Pete Carroll, the Seattle Sea-hawks' head coach, who is famous for taking the unique talents of his players and using them to inform his strategy.

Not only is this approach inclusive and kind, but it's incredibly effective.

LIFE STAGE FIT: ROCK STARS AND SUPER STARS

Not all of us want or need to be on the "fast track," nor do companies want or need everyone to be. As we discussed in the chapter on The Shape of Emotions, depending on our life stage, or the volatility in our home life, we might want work to be boring.

In her book *Radical Candor*, Kim Scott explains the distinction between rock stars and super stars. Rock stars are solid like a rock. They are the dependable workhorses, the utility player who gets the job done—they may be low growth, but they are high performance.[48]

Super stars, by contrast, are the playmakers and risk takers who contribute to high growth and high performance within a business.

TEAMS NEED A MIX

Unfortunately, the way many folks think about growth is often stuck in status conscious ways of thinking. It's assumed that high growth is the same as high status, and that folks who are not on the fast track are worth less.

Historically, underrepresented groups are often pigeonholed into support or leverage roles. For example, "women's work" is assumed to be low status and is generally paid less than the "masculine" equivalents. In corporate America, women are often siloed into marketing or human resources.

As Joanne Lipman points out in her book *That's What She Said*, one of the keys to her success was the luck of having bosses who realized that "kids grow up." While her children were young, she deferred several promotions.[49] In other words she chose to be a rock star.

Instead of writing her off, her bosses understood what she hadn't at the time: that children grow up. Her bosses kept bringing her opportunities. When the time was right, she accepted a super star role and crushed it!

---

48   Kim Scott, Radical Candor (St. Martin's Publishing Group, 2019).
49   Joanne Lipman, That's What She Said (HarperCollins, 2018).

IN SUM

We don't need to feel 100 percent challenged and in the flow to feel happy and engaged at work. There does seem to be a minimum threshold of about 20 percent. In a study from the Mayo Clinic, they found that doctors who experienced just 20 percent of flow at work were less likely to burn out. Twenty percent seems to be the magic number with progressive companies, in industries that put a premium on talent retention, like SONY and Google, which support up to 20 percent of time for personal projects.

Cal Newport in his book *Deep Work* suggests that as we mature in our career, we should target a minimum of 50 percent Deep Work.[50] Newport defines this work separately from flow, although they may overlap. Deep Work is work that is at the top of license, the work that we are best able to do.

Realistically, not all jobs will offer us the best fit between our skills and challenges. However, many jobs could be crafted to be better matches. Both individuals and organizations would be well served to have intentional conversations about fit and match quality. Otherwise, the default tends to win. You may be in an organization where Firecrackers and Spartans tend to claim the "glamorous" opportunities. Alternatively, if your organization is mostly full of Minervas, Firecrackers may get frustrated when the organization refuses to take risks, or are too controlling, and the organization may miss out on new opportunities.

---

50   Cal Newport, Deep Work, (Grand Central Publishing, 2016).

CHAPTER NINE

CLARITY

———

"Nothing in life is to be feared, it is only to be understood. Now is the time to understand more, so that we may fear less."

—ATTRIBUTED TO MARIE CURIE

Clarity is defined as the quality of being easy to see, transparent, and certain. One archaic meaning of the word is glory and "divine splendor," as in knowing the glory of God—the feeling of divinity.

With this in mind, is it any wonder that we seek it?

"The reason it is possible to achieve such complete involvement in a flow experience is that goals are usually clear," Csikszentmihalyi writes in his book *Flow.*[51]

Progressive companies are intentionally transparent about information and goals. There are risks, of course, to that sort of transparency, but those risks are offset, at least in

---

51   Mihaly Csikszentmihalyi, Flow (Harper Perennial, New York, 2008), page 54.

theory, by the gains in performance. We know that intrinsically motivated people—the kind of creative thinkers we increasingly want to lead our organizations—want to feel aligned with the goals of a company. We intuitively understand that alignment creates power and efficiency.

Sharing information also creates trust and communicates respect. Having a clear sense of direction and clear understanding of the goals reduces second-guessing and allows people to make the best decisions for managing their energy and attention.

CLEARLY AMBIGUOUS

Clarity does not necessarily mean simple or straightforward. Between automation and off-shoring, companies are actively devaluing *algorithmic* labor, that is to say the kind of tasks that have a clearly defined solution and place a premium on *heuristic* work—the kind of tasks that have multiple solutions and require creative human problem solving.

I was talking about the role of clarity with a creative lead at a New York-based design firm.

"I don't think clarity is always possible. In fact, getting clarity from the client is a big part of my job," she argued. From her experience, clients don't always know what they need, or they have conflicting stakeholder needs. There is an art to connecting with clients, earning their trust, and going behind the first, second, and even the third ask to make sure the work delivers on both conscious and unconscious goals.

"Clarity does not mean unambiguous," I agreed, "but it can mean being clear about the level of ambiguity and being clear how the process involves wayfinding and creating."

"One hundred percent," she agreed.

FIND THE BALANCE IN THE MESS

We also both agreed that very little is more demoralizing than a client who asks you to be creative, then proceeds to give an extremely prescriptive scope, crushing all enthusiasm. I've worked with designers, developers, and coders, all of whom are creative in their own way. Finding that right balance to trust each other to do their job can be messy.

If the brief is too detailed, a creative will get bored. Too much clarity is like asking a master artist to paint by numbers. It can also be perceived as condescending and frustrating, not to mention a waste of resources.

Conversely, when the brief is too vague, or in the vein of "I'll know it when I see it," the creative team might feel like they are being sent on a wild goose chase.

This is so common an experience for freelance creatives that the website Clients from Hell has devoted numerous entries to the challenges of finding this balance. That said, it could also be exactly what the employee wants in a job. Perhaps you have a young Albert Einstein who wants an easy mindless paycheck while he contemplates the theory of relativity.

That's why trust and communication will never go out of style!

CLARITY FROM ACTION

Creatives and designers know that sometimes, we don't know how things are going to work out—until they do. We don't know what's around the corner until we get there, or what's over the bridge until we cross it.

Experimentation and practice are all ways we get clarity and data. We test and iterate based on what happens.

"Bias to action" is a pillar of having a growth mindset. We can only take an idea so far inside our head. Fellow introverts, I feel you resisting this, but trust me it's not so bad.

At some point, we have to launch. It's the experience and the feeling of pushing past our discomfort, showing up, flipping the coin, pulling the lever on the slot machine, and getting rejected that often teaches us the most. It moves an idea from our head into reality. This is also true for practicing a new habit or launching a new product.

CLARITY AND THE JOY OF LINGO

When working with others, clarity requires communication, understanding, and trust. In this fast-paced world, we crave those quick bursts of connection.

When you work with someone often, you can develop an almost telepathic shorthand. I'm reminded of that scene in *Ocean's Eleven*.[52]

---

52 Ocean's Eleven, directed by Steven Soderbergh, Warner Bros, USA 2001.

RUSTY: You'd need at least a dozen guys, doing a combination of cons.

DANNY: Like what, you think?

RUSTY: Well, off the top of my head, I'd say you're looking at a Boesky, a Jim Brown, a Miss Daisy, two Jethros, and a Leon Spinks. Oh, and the biggest Ella Fitzgerald ever.

Listening to the snappy patter in that sequence, the audience may not understand exactly what is being said but we're impressed. It's just one example of how sympatico Rusty and Danny are. We do this in the corporate world too, casually bandying about terms like SOX, FDIC, AML, SEC, FCC... and make sure to file those TPS reports in triplicate!

Of course, con artist lingo is more fun than the initialisms from corporate finance, but this mental shorthand creates clear efficiency.

WAX ON, WAX OFF

THE DECLINE OF DEFERENCE
In the 1984 *The Karate Kid*, Daniel is accepted for martial arts training by Mr. Miyagi. At first, instead of learning how to fight, he is given a series of chores. This includes famously waxing cars in a very specific fashion.

After several days of this menial labor, Daniel is angry and frustrated and he tells his sensei off, believing that he is being duped. Suddenly, Mr. Miyagi attacks him, and Daniel quickly deflects using the same motions of wax on and wax off. We realize the purpose of all the hard work was to build his strength and reflexes, and we applaud Mr. Miyagi's ingenious teaching methods.

The lesson is, perhaps, we ought to trust and respect our elders. It's unexpected, dramatic, and entertaining. As you may know from your screenwriting 101 class, the source of drama comes from conflict. Our job is about getting stuff done, and this means minimizing conflict, communicating, and building trust. Expecting deference runs counter to this.

Based on a multitude of hit pieces written about millennials, "kids these days" are far less deferential to previous generations. The assumption that leaders and our elders "know better" has been declining steadily since the silent generation.[53]

I haven't watched the *Karate Kid* remake, but I can't imagine that the same scene would work as well today. We're transitioning from generations that prioritize labor and consumption to generations that prioritize sustainability and stewardship. Younger generations are often skeptical of an elder's motivations and assumptions. They want clarity. They don't take as much on faith nor are they willing to defer their own needs to older generations who have demonstrated poor stewardship.

---

53 Bernard Salt, Beyond the Baby Boomers: The Rise of Gen Y, KPMG International, 2007.

Leaders are leaders in no small part because they have a vision that followers buy into. Their followers trust their vision and have confidence in their plan to get there.

SUMMING UP

Lack of clarity often feels stressful and frustrating, like wandering in a dense fog or in a dark room. We follow those who have a clear vision, plan, or process, a metaphorical flashlight that gives us the confidence to move forward. We want to trust and connect and we want the level of bromance we see in *Ocean's Eleven*—to put ourselves in the hands of our sensei but know that trust also has to be earned.

The only feeling that is worse than being in the dark is feeling like we are alone in the dark, stuck with leaders, clients, and co-workers who don't share their light with us. Information is power, and some folks use their position as gatekeepers to information to maintain their own position.

To navigate this, we can cultivate mentors. We also must learn to trust our intuition. We meditate so we can develop somatic, bodily alerts—our internal mirror—reflecting and making sense of the past, but also so that we can be clear in the present moment.

It may be woo-woo, but it works. When we get good at listening to our elephant or gut, our rider or cognitive brain asks better questions and, in turn, can ask for clarity quickly and with confidence.

CHAPTER TEN

FEEDBACK

FEEDBACK IS A GIFT

Anytime someone engages with our work, giving us their attention, we should consider it a gift. Feedback is a mirror, however imperfect or distorted. It can help us discover missing holes, gaps in our understanding, and blind spots. It can also offer us new opportunities to connect and understand each other. This exchange should never be taken for granted.

Like all gifts, however, it is best to accept feedback gracefully. That said, while we must accept it, we don't always need to take it out of the box, much less use it.

I watched a clip of Gary Vaynerchuk, CEO of VaynerMedia, and Ray Dalio, CEO of Bridgewater, talking about how much they enjoy negative, almost brutal feedback.[54]

---

54 Gary Vaynerchuk, "Ray Dalio, Principles: the Evolution of Bridgewater Associates, & Meditation," #AskGaryVee, Episode 275, December 6, 2017.

First, let me point out that these men are a bit OG. They have a lot of experience f**ing up in public, brushing themselves off, and getting back up. I aspire to that level of DGAFery, and I know there are a lot of painful mistakes that lay between where I am now and where those guys are. Also, I'm not a masochist, and unlike those weirdos, I can't say I'm looking forward to it.

When we are just starting out, it is okay not to be open to unfiltered feedback. We are often told to "toughen up."

I don't agree. It's okay; in fact, it's perfectly reasonable to not have a

"THICK SKIN"

I was discussing this with my friend Sela Lewis, an amazing design strategist with a background in graphic design, about her idea of the right level of feedback.

Sela loves the fire hose. She's experienced dealing with brutal peer critique sessions, a skill she developed in art school. Good, bad, indifferent, she can find gold in it all.

If you can do that, that is awesome!

A "thick skin" just isn't the right metaphor for everyone. Some research shows that some folks, particularly empaths and intuitives, just feel more deeply. What that means is that they take negative feedback much more to heart.

These are the folks who have heard "you're too sensitive" all their lives. In the right context, empathy, intuition, and sensitivity are pure magic. It is a strength and should be managed intelligently, not ignored, bottled up, or numbed. If not modulated correctly, blunt and harsh feedback is counterproductive.

Below is a strategy if you can't or simply don't want to deal with the feedback fire hose.

PRIORITIZE THE FEEDBACK THAT MATTERS.

Twyla Tharp, the choreographer goddess in *The Creative Habit*, describes her process. She intentionally cultivates a select group of people based on their taste and discernment. These people understand her work and her vision. She has learned over time that they are the only ones that matter.

Elizabeth Gilbert, eater, prayer, lover, and author of several best-selling books, in an article for *O* magazine, shared similar questions she asks when seeking feedback:

- Do I trust this person's taste and judgment? AND
- Does this person understand what I'm trying to create here? AND
- Does this person genuinely want me to succeed? AND
- Is this person capable of delivering the truth to me in a sensitive and compassionate manner?

MY MOM: CHEERLEADER AND CRITIC

Gilbert's list stuck with me. I found her list after my final attempt to share a draft of a novel with my mom. A little background: My mother has, for most of my life, been my biggest cheerleader, at least when it came to my career and school.

She is also a creative artist. I grew up admiring her oil paintings from her high school art class and super ornate egg designs every Easter. She's also the reason I'm a science fiction-loving anglophile and creative. We used to binge on Merchant Ivory films and Masterpiece miniseries before binging was a thing. Growing up, fantastical paperbacks from Anthony's Xanth series to McCaffery's Pern littered our apartment and my imagination.

We have a lot of the same tastes and I shared my writing with her because I genuinely hoped she'd enjoy it. I assumed she'd get it and I knew she wanted me to succeed more than anyone. Because of this, I assumed she would be able to give me good, useful feedback and encourage me to keep going.

She did not.

Her feedback was callous and cutting—all negatives, no positives.

Okay, this is a bit embarrassing to admit. If I was acting like a self-aware adult who studies and teaches mindfulness, I would have thanked her and that would have been that.

That is not what happened.

Her response triggered my own not so pretty and, frankly, crappy feedback about *her* feedback. In short, I decided I would be the bigger jerk. Now, being a jerk is not an actual Olympic sport, but if it was, I'm pretty sure I could medal.

Yes, I've read *The Artist's Way* several times and yes, I am aware of the pitfalls of working with frustrated artists. Yes,

I was aware that she'd stopped painting years ago and how with her recent knee replacement, she'd been forced to give up gardening, her main creative outlet.

Unfortunately, I remembered all this after I stopped acting like an overgrown baby. It was obvious in retrospect that her feedback was an outlet for her own creative frustrations. It wasn't about me. It wasn't personal.

Damned if I could get there in the moment. I was in full elephant brain mode, defaulting to what I had been expecting and what I thought I needed.

Our families are our living past, our roots, where we've come from, where we've been. Roots are also muddy, dirty, and messy. We have to handle them with care and love. All that to say...

Let's be kind to our moms and ourselves.

We're all doing the best we can. And seriously, please learn from me If this ever happens to you, with any loved one, just say thank you.

ESCAPING THE VOID
Not getting feedback and being ignored is painful.

Timely feedback communicates quality, attention, and value. Not receiving feedback in a timely manner can generate both anxiety and boredom. This drains us of energy and motivation and may make us feel excluded and like we don't belong. Feedback functions like a mirror. It makes the work go faster and amplifies it. The absence of feedback can feel like a drain.

STILL FACE BABY EXPERIMENT

Feedback is not simply necessary for course correcting and doing good work. It is how humans are wired. Stern, withholding, exclusionary managers remind me of the Still Face Baby experiment.[55] In experiments with infants, scientists asked mothers to briefly not respond at all to their baby, presenting a "blank face." In videos of these experiments, you can see how the baby reacts. At first the baby is puzzled and does cute stuff to get her mom's attention.

If the cooing infant could talk, it would probably be saying, "Hey Mom, what's up? Is something wrong? What's with the resting mom face? Okay, now you look creepy, stop staring at me, is there something wrong because I'm really freaking out. You look scarier than the chick who climbs out of the TV. If you don't stop this, I'm going to scream...," and cue the wailing.

We are social creatures, wired for social feedback. A lack of feedback leaves us feeling like we are wasting our time, aimless, going down a rabbit hole, or that our work is not valued.

Some managers complain that workers who request feedback are "needy" or entitled members of a pampered spoiled

---

55 University of Massachusetts, Boston, "Still Face Experiment: Dr. Edward Tronick." November 20, 2008.

generation. That said, we know that feedback is essential for deliberate practice, the specific kind of practice needed to achieve mastery.

It's not needy or entitled to want to grow. New research suggests we should actively apply the

80:20 POSITIVE TO NEGATIVE RULE

In *Nine Lies About Work,* strengths-based consultants Marcus Buckingham and Ashley Goodall shared new research that suggests employees benefit from feedback that roughly follows the buoyancy ratio.[56]We'll unpack buoyancy more fully in Part Three when we discuss psychological buoyancy and paradox. The important thing to take away is that most people appreciate when we acknowledge their talents and what they do well. It makes them feel seen, recognized, and understood. Buckingham suggests managers should actively seek out those bright spots to "catch" folks in the act of being awesome and encourage them to keep it up. It's basic positive psychology.

Consider the situation where a teenager is drinking out of the milk jug and a parent wants to discourage this bad habit.

- Scenario one: we yell at her every time we catch her doing it.
- Scenario two: we acknowledge and thank her when she uses a glass.

---

56 Marcus Buckingham and Ashley Goodall, Nine Lies About Work (Harvard Business Review Press, 2019).

Now let's ask ourselves:

- Which one of these two scenarios *feels* better to the teenager?
- Which one feels better to the parent?
- Which one is more likely to succeed?
- Which one are we more likely to do?

Most people intuit correctly that positive reinforcement works best, and also reluctantly admit that we are more likely to scold or shame the bad behavior.

Our brains are wired to alert us to problems rather than the good things. Which means we are more likely to be triggered by mistakes and give negative feedback rather than positive encouragement.

By the way, you are not a monster if you give negative feedback. That's how many of us were raised and it's really hard to model new ways of being and break the cycle. Truthfully, you turned out okay, so give yourself a break and perhaps practice a little self-compassion.

We're always learning new things. As Maya Angelou reminds us, we do the best we can, until we learn better, and when we learn better, we do better.

IN SHORT

Feedback is not a "nice to have" or an entitlement. It's a real need. It also makes sense that we learn how to give it constructively and in a way that creates energy.

CHAPTER ELEVEN

CONTROL

"The more we value things outside our control the less control we have."

—EPICTETUS

Csikszentmihalyi writes about "the paradox of control," describing it as the *feeling* of controlling outcomes rather than actually *being* able to control outcomes. It *feels* like being in control, which stops us worrying about losing control.[57]

This paradox is enticing, existing at the edge of our capability and balancing our human drive for both certainty and variety.[58] Enjoyment comes not just from the danger or uncertainty but the ability to master it. Flow feels and looks effortless, but part of that is because of all the effortful practice beforehand that makes something look easy.

---

57 Mihaly Csikszentmihalyi, Flow (Harper Perennial, New York, 2008).
58 Team Tony, "6 Human Needs: Do You Need to Feel Significant?" Tonyrobbins.com.

If Flow is like flying, we don't master it by gripping the controls with all our strength. We have to trust the process. We trust our training and experience. We trust physics and invisible air currents to hold us up. That is how we learn to soar.[59]

FOCUS ON WHAT YOU CAN CONTROL

"If a problem is fixable, if a situation is such that you can do something about it, then there is no need to worry. If it's not fixable, then there is no help in worrying. There is no benefit in worrying whatsoever."

—DALAI LAMA XIV

Focusing on what we can control is a coaching mantra.

Things we can't control: our parents, the weather, election results, squirrels eating tomatoes, the stock market, our customers, our kids, our dad's fashion sense, the *Game of Thrones* ending.

Things we can control: ourselves (sort of).

You may be thinking, "But I can sell ice to a snow man, and I can read the market like it's no one's business, and my kid does what I tell her to do all the time. I am a master of control."

Slow your roll, madam. Don't confuse influence, luck, and the fact that your kid is an oddball with control. Controlling

---

59 Anecdotally, flying a plane, hang gliding, BASE jumping, skydiving, and other gravity-defying activities seem to be correlated with Flow.

ourselves, our effort, our decisions, and where we invest our time, energy, and money is actually often enough to get what we want in life.

As in the earlier story with Leslie Odom, Jr., we may not be able to control the game, but we can control our commitment to our craft. We can control our decision to take care of ourselves and show up with our full energetic self.

BURNOUT AND THE LOSS OF CONTROL

"Research shows that one of the major causes of burnout is a lack of efficacy, feeling incapable of making an impact."[60]

—ADAM GRANT

When we treat people like automatons, we get automatons. Being an order taker and following the rules may be expected at the beginning of our career, but research has shown that to activate intrinsic motivation, people need autonomy.

Nowhere is this more obvious than in the creative process. Some companies establish rigid style guides, templates, and rules, which reduce designers to desktop layout technicians. It's disempowering, demoralizing, and, in my opinion, a waste of talent.

As Patty McCord says in her 2015 TED Talk, "there is no magic empowerment wand. People are naturally powerful.

---

60 Adam Grant (host), "Burnout Is Everyone's Problem" WorkLife with Adam Grant, March 2020,

The problem is organizational structures designed to block and stymy that power."[61]

"There is nothing worse than being blocked from your purpose," Hacking HR founder Enrique Rubio told me when I interviewed him about his experience starting up the Hacking HR global movement. Hacking HR started when Rubio created a space for HR professionals interested in making the workplace more human to come together, connect, and support each other. Unfortunately, his bosses at the time were not supportive of his side project's success. Despite creating a unique opportunity to showcase his organization, they did not want anything to do with it. Like the story with Larry Page, it wasn't the way things were done and they strongly suggested Rubio should put an end to it.

"How did you deal with that?" I asked.

"As best I could, but I couldn't quit. There was clearly such a global need for the community, so eventually I had to leave," he told me, admitting it felt like a risk leaving a stable career with a prestigious organization. Fortunately, since then Hacking HR has only grown in size and scale, hosting over two thousand events, webinars, virtual conferences for over one hundred thousand HR professionals in over eighty-five cities around the world, inspiring folks in the field of people development to step up and make a difference.

Many of us crave autonomy and enjoy the process of figuring things out and generating delight. When those in charge

---

61   Patty McCord, "HR lessons from the world of Silicon Valley start-ups" *TED*, June 2015.

block that from happening, it destroys not just good ideas, but it also destroys motivation.

Almost as bad as not having any control of one's work is having one's work completely ignored, overwritten, and discarded. Leaders can't establish trust if they don't actually need or value other people's work. There is nothing more demoralizing than when someone says, "Get out of the way, I'll just do it myself."

In fact, the most rational efficient response to being pushed aside is to mentally check out. It's not necessarily a signal of inherent laziness or apathy, it may be a sign that one does not feel valued. Even when we know that the leader is just stressed, or a perfectionist, it's difficult not to take such treatment personally. In the moment, such behavior often feels disrespectful and contemptuous, although it may also be a sign that the leader is burning out.

People with talent and options don't stay in those situations for long.

It's painful when a boss, non-creative leader, or client "tweaks" and dilutes something that came out brilliant and pure. One client refers to this as "creativity by committee," and it is the bane of his existence.

Creative professionals aren't delusional; they understand that the folks with money have the final decision-making power. Like with everything, though, it's a balance and a negotiation. When we dismiss a creative or expert's input often enough, she'll either check out or burn out.

OUR INNER SPIRIT ANIMAL

When my dog got kicked out of doggie daycare for barking and snapping at other dogs, I was upset and offended on his behalf.

"What do you mean my baby is not well-behaved? He's not that way with me!"

We'd done some dog training and he was pretty well-behaved at home and at the dog park. With me, he very rarely even barked, and I'd only seen him snap at another dog once—an annoying Collie who kept snapping at his heels and, frankly, had it coming.

After speaking to another dog trainer, she told me that my pup probably just didn't like doggie day care. "For some dogs it's too stimulating, and it's completely natural for them to outgrow it." Basically, my dog gets cranky in crowds, and would rather be at home cuddled up in bed.

That's my boy!

NOT SO DEEP DOWN, WE'RE ALL ANIMALS

After researching habit formation and motivation, it's impossible not to make the connection between training dogs and training ourselves. Biologically, we're designed to react to stimulus. It's what keeps us alive. Worrying and stressing is healthy and has a purpose.

According to Sheena Iyengar's book *The Art of Choosing*, when we are unable to exert control it creates stress. Under duress, the endocrine system produces stress hormones, such as adrenaline, that prepare the body to deal with immediate danger—the good old "fight or flight" response.[62]

The fear response's biological purpose is for short-term sprints. Stress is intended to motivate us to deal with the source of anxiety and regain "control" as quickly as possible. However, chronic stress leaves us exhausted, wiped out, and depleted. Left unchecked, stress can kill us. Because of this, Iyengar writes, animals in captivity have shorter life expectancies. Similarly, she found that the less control people had over their work, the higher their blood pressure during working hours.

LOOSENING OUR GRIP

"Under pressure, when we're concerned about performing at our best, we can try and control aspects of what we're doing that should be left outside conscious control. The end result is that we mess up."

—SIAN LEAH BEILOCK, TEDMED 2017[63]

Understanding what to control and what to automate takes practice. In sports, we have to trust our practice and muscle memory. We have to trust our teammates and have faith in the process.

Worrying about the outcome and the things outside of our control—our competition, the wind, and so on—can be low value and counter-effective.

---

62 Sheena Iyengar, The Art of Choosing (Twelve Publishing, 2011).
63 Sian Leah Beilock, "Why We Choke Under Pressure—and How to Avoid it." TEDMED 2017, November 2017.

CONTROL IS A COMFORTING ILLUSION

We waste energy and attention worrying about things outside of our control, rather than assessing the probabilities and deciding how we will act. Feeling worried, i.e. when we are in the upper left hand quadrant of the match quality grid, is a good indicator that our attention is stuck on something outside our control. Many of us hold on too tight. We fight and resist when we might be better served by relaxing, softening, and getting curious about what we can and can't control. Instead of worrying about what might happen, we can make a plan for each contingency. We can get clear about our options so that if the worst does happen, we have a plan ready and can hit the ground running.

CHAPTER TWELVE

FOCUS

"Concentrate all your thoughts upon the work at hand. The sun's rays do not burn until brought to a focus."

—ALEXANDER GRAHAM BELL

When people are in flow, they report that they feel an incredible sense of focus.

In Napoleon Hill's popular wealth book *Think and Grow Rich,* he advises folks to focus on their goal every single day.[64] Warren Buffet is famous for his advice to limit one's focus and ignore second and third-tier priorities because those secondary priorities will thwart your dreams.[65]

If you've read this far, you can probably already guess that there is also such a thing as too much focus. In his book *Drive,* Daniel Pink explains how psychological studies indicate that

---

64 Napoleon Hill, Think and Grow Rich (Jeremy P. Tarcher/Penguin, 2008).

65 Warren Buffet's advice to his pilot can be found in the Inc Article by Jory Mackay, "This Brilliant Strategy Used by Warren Buffett Will Help You Prioritize Your Time," Inc.com, 2017.

extrinsic rewards cause people to hurry and focus, and in so doing actually produce less creative and worse outcomes.[66] When a project requires any sort of non-obvious decision-making, tightening our focus actually creates delays.

The benefits of relaxation and reflection are apparent in the biography of an American luminary. In *My Own Words*, Ruth Bader Ginsburg recalls how her days were divided between school and caring for her newborn. Reading picture books and A.A. Milne poems and bathing and feeding her baby in the evenings allowed her to return to her studies with renewed vigor. Each part of her life was a respite from the other and allowed her a sense of proportion and perspective that others more narrowly focused on the law did not have.[67]

Intentional focusing is like hitting the gas; relaxing is letting your foot off the gas and coasting.[68] The sweet spot, effortless flow and the experience of absorbed attention, is in the balanced tension between relaxation and focus.

A PULSE NOT A PUSH

One of the benefits of living in New York City is that there is always something happening. One evening in late 2012, I found myself at the Yale Club on Vanderbilt Avenue, just

---

66 Daniel H. Pink, Drive (Riverhead Books, 2009).

67 Ruth Bader Ginsburg, and Mary Hartnett, and Wendy W. Willians, My Own Words (New York: Simon & Schuster, 2016).

68 It may be interesting to note that in Tesla vehicles, coasting and taking your foot off the gas actually activates the regenerative braking system. It's a perfect metaphor for finding Flow.

outside Grand Central Station, attending a lecture from Richard Foster, emeritus McKinsey director.

The topic was on the cognitive science of creativity. His findings seemed to indicate that in highly creative people, their thoughts rapidly diverge and converge as they created, finding, joining, and discarding new ideas in random succession.

It was the first time I'd heard another businessperson describe what I *felt* in my bones. At the time I was writing a novel. Figuring out where a story was going was very much like the process he described. It was like solving a puzzle in which we have some of the pieces, some order, and perhaps even an idea of what it looks like in the end. It was a process, diverging to discover the next piece, where my characters would go and converging to fit it in once I figured it out, writing quickly until the gap, the next crossroads. In this way, I slowly found my way through the story.

I discussed this process with Michael J. Sullivan, the bestselling science fiction and fantasy author and creator of dozens of books including the *Riyria Chronicles*. He is incredibly disciplined with his writing, sometimes completing multiple books in a year. It's one of the reasons I admire him and often ask him for advice on both the craft and profession of writing.

He told me that "writing a novel is 100 percent decision-making." That's what the writing process is: figuring out what happens next.

Psychologically, decision-making takes energy—a lot of it. Decisions happen in our reflective mind, what we've previously discussed as our "rider" or conscious brain. This part of the brain requires more energy and processing power than our elephant, automatic, unconscious brain.

What Foster shared was that creativity is not just about converging and making decisions. Flow functions like breathing, inhaling and exhaling, diverging and converging—skimming or surfing between our automatic elephant brain and so-called rational conscious mind.

Most of us are good at using our willpower to consciously focus, tightening our grip. What is less intuitive is the importance of also relaxing our brain. The reasons for this may be that our society pushes for more, more, more, rather than finding balance and quitting when we've had enough.

Understanding the process of when to diverge and when to converge is another fundamental element of having a growth mindset and managing creative projects.

WONDER AND WANDER
Another human-centered design maxim is to avoid getting stuck on gravity problems—things that we cannot change.[69] When we hit a wall and get stuck and can't punch through, it often makes sense to step back, take a breath, and reassess.

Michelle Mahony, senior principal at Daggerwing, understands the power of wandering. "When I really need to get

---

69   Bill Burnett and Dave Evans, Designing Your Life (New York: Alfred A. Knopf, 2016).

creative, I leave my desk and take a walk," she says. When working at her home in Rhode Island, she has access to a state park and practices "forest bathing," which are deeply immersive meditative walks in nature. Even when she is at Daggerwing's offices in midtown Manhattan, she has access to both the ambient inspiration of one of the world's busiest commercial districts as well as the natural tableaus of Central Park. More importantly, she also understands when members of her team need to take a break and trusts when they need to take a walk to find their flow.

Wandering facilitates creative connections that our brain may miss if we are wound too tight.

MULTIPLE AREAS OF FOCUS

The importance of limiting one's focus seems to be the default advice. As more diverse personalities and folks succeed, we're finding that the "rules" for success are far more diverse and nuanced.

A MULTI-PASSIONATE THOUGHT LEADER

In her book *Everything Is Figureoutable*, coaching guru Marie Forleo talks about what a relief it was to come across the term "multi-passionate entrepreneur."[70]

There is a lot of advice about the importance of picking one thing and focusing. When Forleo came across the term

---

70 Marie Forleo, *Everything Is Figureoutable* (New York: Portfolio Books, 2019).

multi-passionate entrepreneur, she was bartending, working as a Nike ambassador, creating fitness videos, and starting up life coaching. Some of what she was doing was generating money in the short term so that she could finance her long-term vision.

As a coach, she knew the value of focusing, but it never *felt like* the right advice for her. Once she came across the term "multi-passionate entrepreneur," it gave her permission to do what worked for her. In her case, it meant going full throttle on multiple projects, even if it meant long-term goals took a bit longer. It was a relief finding the language that articulated what she needed.

SCI-FI TO NONFICTION TO NOIR AND BACK AGAIN

Another person for whom this holds true is one of my favorite authors, Hugo-award winning John Scalzi. Recently I was fortunate enough to meet him in person.

I knew from reading his blog that he had two literary agents, one for fiction and one for nonfiction. Most advice for new authors suggests we focus on one genre. It makes sense to build one audience at a time. Unfortunately, not everyone's brains are so cooperative; at least my brain isn't.[71]

Since I was in the middle of writing this book and already in the habit of asking personal questions, I got over my fangirl

---

71 For context, the last full draft of a book I wrote was a sequel to Pride and Prejudice. Before that I drafted a series of science fiction short stories set in Japan. I did this after writing technical business thought leadership and marketing copy for about ten years.

nerves and asked how he felt about writing in mixed genres. I expected him to scold me and admonish me as a new author to do one thing at a time.

To my delight, he said that he finds that different genres require totally different headspaces. Switching back and forth actually helps him write and recharge for each book.

FROM BROADWAY TO HBO TO IMPROV

In his November 2020 appearance on *The Daily Show*, Lin Manuel Miranda, who you may know as playing Alexander Hamilton to Odom's Aaron Burr, commented that his work on Broadway, doing improvisation in Freestyle Love Supreme, felt like exercising the "opposite muscle" from acting on scripted dramas.[72]

His point is that even though it was demanding work and could have been a distraction from his other projects, the balance worked for him.

DOING MORE TO FOCUS

Finally, in the *WorkLife* podcast, Adam Grant interviewed Conray Callahan, a Philadelphia teacher who found that adding *more* work actually helped her avoid burnout.[73, 74]Spe-

72 The Daily Show with Trevor Noah, Lin-Manuel Miranda—"His Dark Materials" and "Freestyle Love Supreme," YouTube, November 26, 2019.

73 Grant, Adam (host), "Burnout Is Everyone's Problem" WorkLife with Adam Grant, March 2020.

74 Shout out to all the students, staff, and teachers from Black Bottom and University City High School, where I spent a school year from 1998-99 working on school to career placements.

cifically, she added work where she had control, care, and impact—i.e., flow work. That kind of work helped restore her energy, although she admitted, "It sounds counterintuitive, but I felt really refreshed and like I had a renewed sense of purpose and drive."

The takeaway is that the "correct" number of projects to focus on depends on the work and how the person performing the tasks feels. Sometimes less is more, and sometimes more is more. What differentiates the two is how we feel.

THE POINT

Finding the right amount of focus can be a tricky balance. It helps to understand that it *is* a balance and it may require experimentation to figure out what works for us. We need to default to driving forward, but almost as important is learning to trust ourselves to back off and relax, which often feels counterintuitive.

CHAPTER THIRTEEN

EVERYDAY LIFE
FALLS AWAY

───

The removal of distractions can facilitate focus and deep concentration and, like many of the ideas we discuss, this rule is not an absolute. Some people do their best work in a cafe with its ambient noise and micro distractions. Some need absolute silence and some folks grab their headphones and pump up the volume.

The most obvious threat to good work is

THE DISTRACTION ECONOMY

The distraction economy is also known as the attention economy. As a practitioner and facilitator of meditation, I'm increasingly conscious of how we give away our attention. We thoughtlessly allow other people to access and control our emotions and energy. If you've ever spent more than five minutes responding to a rant on Facebook or have let a stupid news article put you in a bad mood, you've been mentally hijacked by the distraction economy.

It may be comforting to know that almost everyone, including myself, has experienced this.

DIGITAL MINIMALISM

In his books *Deep Work* and *Digital Minimalism*, Cal Newport shares that the digital tools we use were created to intentionally steal our attention.[75] Face it: really smart psychologists, programmers, and marketers working at Facebook, Apple, Google, and Microsoft are paid a lot of money to figure out how to snag our attention. The more of our attention, clicks, and eyeball time we give, the more advertising revenue they get and the higher their stock price goes. This is not a secret. We're just one person against the machine of capitalism.

Silicon Valley executives create boundaries for their own children, with strict limits on what they are allowed to watch and for how long.[76] They understand that kids are basically underdeveloped sociopathic puppies and aren't equipped to regulate their emotions and awareness for themselves.[77]

Honestly, neither are most of us adults.

---

75 Cal Newport, Digital Minimalism (Portfolio/Penguin, 2019).
76 Nellie Bowles, "A Dark Consensus About Screens and Kids Begins to Emerge in Silicon Valley," New York Times, October 26, 2018.
77 Obviously, I don't have kids. For my friends with kids, please don't get your knickers in a bunch. I'm not talking about your kids. Your kids are great. It's other people's kids that are the problem, obviously, winky face.

Silicon Valley is well aware of how addictive its technology is and knows that there are real, unstudied risks to unchecked technological use. That's why they limit their own families' use of tech. My guess is that once the cognitive risks are better understood, we'll see these technologies, either through regulation or user demand, offer more enhancements for people to set better boundaries and limits.

It may not be able to stop us from binging the entire season of *Altered Carbon* as soon as it drops. But the technology can nudge and alert us that doing so might not be in our best interest.[78]

Practicing metacognition and awareness helps us practice being intentional about what we give our attention to. Sometimes just a breath or pause can help us break the habit cycle.

EMAIL PING PONG AND THE LOWEST COMMON DENOMINATOR
Email is another wonderful digital illustration of how our energy can get sucked down into these recursive, reactionary loops.

Much of how we act is relational; we mirror habits, customs, and behavior, defaulting to social norms. This is why we often get caught up in feedback loops when we don't create intentional habits and norms around how we use technology.

---

78 I can probably quit anytime I want. For a primer on libertarian paternalism, and how we can ignore Netflix's suggestions to get a life, use choice architecture for good not evil, check out Nudge by Sunstein and Thaler.

For example, some folks prioritize speedy responses over thoughtful, intentional replies. Sometimes this is because they intend to signal responsiveness. Sometimes they are abdicating responsibility by throwing the ball back into someone else's court, not bothering to read the full email. This may mean they miss important points, which can have negative downstream effects and create unnecessary email clutter.

Get clear on appropriate email etiquette and the level of attention that needs to be given to the email and by whom. You can almost feel the energy from an email, both the level of attention and intention, from the passive aggressive "as previously written," to the outright aggressive ALL CAPS RESPONSE, to the dismissive and contemptuous "k."

Comedians joke that the person who cares less in a relationship has the most power.

Email tussles definitely seem to illustrate this dynamic.

ONE SIMPLE WAY TO GET LESS EMAIL? SEND FEWER EMAILS

It may also help to communicate both our intention and boundaries. For example, one executive I work with has an auto responder, explaining that she will only be reviewing emails at certain times of the day. Their organization's culture also supports not jumping at every single email. Her auto responder also clarifies reasonable expectations on her time and attention.

Such boundaries may be especially important when we feel like we are working with others who are hyper reactionary and thoughtless.

WORK-LIFE SILO

"I get asked about work-life balance all the time. And my view is, that's a debilitating phrase because it implies there's a strict trade-off."

—JEFF BEZOS[79]

There is a fair bit of advice on how to focus and remove distraction. Our default seems to be to urge folks to converge and focus. The ancients might comment that convergence, focusing and coming to the point, is very masculine or yang.

Neuroscience seems to show that men's brains are better at focusing as opposed to lateral thinking. Focus modes of thinking are generally considered the "norm." Men are rewarded for being goal-oriented and are permitted to have tunnel vision. They are rewarded even for being cutthroat, since they are the closers—and everyone knows coffee is for closers. Studies show that men are traditionally better at ultimatums—transactional one-time-only negotiations. That's generalized, of course. As the social distinction between genders blur, people are finding a new internal balance between being sharp and focused with being flexible and accommodating.

Women are taught to put their short-term needs aside and put relationships first. Women are more likely to be taught that their power comes from being liked and protected, rather than their competency. As women are busting that limiting

---

79 Zoë Bernard, "Jeff Bezos' Advice to Amazon Employees Is to Stop Aiming for Work-Life 'Balance'—Here's What You Should Strive for Instead," *Business Insider*, January 9, 2019.

false dichotomy, men are learning that to rise to the next level of leadership. They need to start caring, empathizing and thinking about the long-term.

WOMEN AND BABIES

In *Flow*, Csikszentmihalyi indicates that some new mothers actually enjoy returning to work. Many of them report that when they are at home, they have about six things on their mind, from their children's crying, phone calls, mommy dates, a messy house, dogs, errands, playground politics, etc. By comparison, the office can be a relatively distraction-free zone and a pleasant break from the chaotic responsibility of their domestic duties.

Work-life balance is not as simple as it sounds—it shifts and evolves. Jeff Bezos and Michelle Obama have both publicly commented that it's sometimes not possible to have both at the same time. They, along with Ginsburg as mentioned in the previous chapter, as well as Sallie Krawcheck from the introduction, have all publically commented on how domestic duties can actually provide a space to process and absorb the day's lessons.

MONEY, POVERTY, AND DEBTS AS DISTRACTIONS

I must acknowledge that all these folks have extraordinary resources that give them the control, flexibility, and support to work around conflicts. Ginsburg, for example, wrote about having a nanny in addition to having a supportive life partner. Money and our short-term physical needs are some of the biggest weights and distractions pulling against our long-term, creative vision and energy.

We're only starting to understand and acknowledge the stress and insecurity created by student loans, debt, and wage inequality and how all of this perpetuates status inequity. In the short term, many students report feeling stressed, worried, and distracted by the weight of insurmountable student loans debts. For some it feels like a literal weight, holding them back from taking career risks and non-traditional opportunities.

For those in debt, or with limited resources, the struggle is real. Mindfulness can help with buoyancy and resetting our emotional compass, but it takes real energy and should not be taken for granted.

CREATE A PATH FREE FROM DISTRACTIONS

I first heard the term "create the path" reading Dan and Chip Heath's book *Switch*.[80]

It's similar to the idea of "setting someone up for success," which is a trick I learned while training my dog, Remy. In puppy training, we learned that dogs respond better to positive reinforcement.

It helps to start in a low distraction environment and make it easy for our pups to succeed early and often. Setting my dog up for success also meant changing myself

---

80 Chip Heath and Dan Heath, Switch (New York: Broadway Books, 2010).

as much as my dog. It wasn't fair to take him to the dog park where he was likely to be overstimulated. Instead, we worked on training his attention at home before adding outside distractions.

Setting him up for success meant changing my behavior as much as his. For example, I learned I had to be better at putting the lid on the trash and not to leave things lying around that he wants to chew on, like my favorite coral pumps. Instead, I take him to places where he can appropriately channel his energy.

It's much the same for our inner elephant. Our rider, or conscious brain, only has so much energy to control our elephant. One trick highly productive people use is that they "automate their grit and willpower" by creating routines and processes to set them up to get the necessary distractions out of the way.

A great example of this is from Twyla Tharp. In her book *Creative Habit*, she writes how she begins each day by getting into a taxi to take her to the studio in the morning.[81] Like getting on a roller coaster, once she gets in the cab she doesn't have a choice. She begins her ritual, which leads her into her creative flow.

Many writers do something similar, such as sitting down at a certain time everyday, butt in chair, with no Wi-Fi and no option other than writing or staring out the window.

---

81   Twyla Tharp, The Creative Habit (New York: Simon & Schuster, 2003).

THE TAKEAWAY

Keep showing up. Our process evolves and is often somewhat idiosyncratic. We start with cultivating an awareness of what tugs at our energy, what uniquely makes us tick, what we need and what we want. We can be mindful to set boundaries and prepare to communicate and negotiate for what we need.

A corollary to this is to respect other people's boundaries. Awesome folks with healthy boundaries respect and are accountable for honoring other people's boundaries. Be that awesome person and look for it in others. Invariably, those are also the people we can trust and rely upon.

CHAPTER FOURTEEN

SELFLESS

"The two biggest barriers to good decision making are your ego and your blind spots."

—RAY DALIO[82]

"Whenever I hit an obstacle, I step back and check my ego," Peter Madigan tells me.[83] We're having coffee at Peet's Coffee in Shirlington Village, where we often meet to shoot the breeze about business, life, Zen, and leadership lessons. Madigan's wife, Megan, introduced us after hearing me talk about how yoga relates to business and game theory and we've been friends ever since.

Madigan worked for sixteen years as a political consultant and partner before retiring as president of Peck, Madigan, Jones & Stewart. He now teaches leadership for the University of Maine. Like me, he is a total business nerd. I'm fascinated at how he found success working with

---

82 Ray Dalio, Principles: Life and Work (New York: Simon & Schuster, 2017).

83 Peter Madigan, Interviewed August 6, 2019.

Capitol Hill, consulting in one of the most old-school power bastions.

Madigan looks a bit like if we crossed Paul Newman from the 1986 movie *The Color of Money* with General David Petraeus. Clean cut and blue-eyed, he's down-to-earth and affable, which makes sense considering he's negotiated around some of the biggest egos in politics for most of his career. It didn't take me long to discover that he has a unique gift for being inquisitive and even disagreeable, without giving offense. What's his secret?

"IT'S NEVER ABOUT ME"

"It really isn't," he says. He admits he didn't always feel that way, but with age comes something akin to wisdom. He talks a lot about the importance of being client focused. It's obvious this is at the core of his beliefs.

I'll note, he had the advantage of playing the game on the default settings: white and male. Something he himself acknowledges is a growing understanding from the perspective of having a wife, who is also a business owner, as well as a daughter, who just graduated from Dickinson. It has given him some insight and empathy into their different experiences. Early on in our chats, we discovered we share a similar work ethic, his obtained growing up the youngest of seven with three older sisters and depression-era parents who taught them to take nothing for granted. Both of us have had to negotiate similar status issues, something that is not always respected or understood by those with old money and power.

The truth is, everyone has obstacles. We all have to play the game handed to us and set our ego aside. He learned this lesson early in his career.

"A while back, I was shepherding a client, a Detroit automaker, through a meeting with Trent Lott, who was the Senate Majority leader at the time," he tells me, explaining that the senator was "a true gentleman of the South, who knew I was from Maine."

At that point, Madigan felt like he had a solid relationship with the senator's office, partly due to an encyclopedic binder of information about the senator's preferences and idiosyncrasies. One of these notes included Senator Lott's strong dislike of facial hair—a fact he unfortunately recalled about two minutes into this particular meeting.

"I'm not sure why I even had a beard, I was probably just trying it out and it totally slipped my mind, until I saw the senator looking at me funny." Madigan shakes his head and I can tell he still feels a bit of chagrin at the memory.

Fortunately, he had the presence of mind to come up with a cover, just before the senator stopped the meeting.

"Peter what's with the—," Lott asked, gesturing to his own chin, indicating his beard.

Without missing a beat Madigan replied, "Yes, sir. The beard. I'm in a Civil War re-enactment this weekend. But don't worry, I die in the first charge."

The Senator surveyed him for a moment, a small scowl on his face, as if trying to decide whether to accept this neat fiction, but nodded with a brief "very good."

Madigan's answer may have been barely plausible, but it showed he understood the Senator and was appropriately deferential. He was able to succinctly communicate that even if they weren't on the same side of the Civil War, Madigan was a team player.

He also shaved the beard.

LEADERSHIP LESSONS—HOW TO CREATE TRUST
"If you want to go fast, go alone. If you want to go far, go together."

—AFRICAN PROVERB

Success comes down to creating and cultivating trust and connection and feeling safe and understood. Madigan understood early on that his job was to help, and to do that, he had to be trusted.

"People want to tell you what they want all the time, but most consultants don't want to listen and hear the client's problems," Madigan tells me, and then shares his

FIVE CRITICAL QUALITIES FOR
CREATING TRUST AS A CONSULTANT

1. **Empathy.** Being able to take another's perspective and to relate to our client is a no-brainer. We have to be able "take their side" and understand where they are coming from.

2. **Self-Awareness.** This includes emotional intelligence and psychological distance. A lot of consultants, especially early on in their careers, make things about themselves and what they want to sell. They lack the self-awareness to even notice when they are doing this and can put a lot of clients off.

3. **Decisiveness.** Part of being decisive is being prepared, having contingency plans, and focusing on what we can control. Practice and experience can play a role in this capability. Clients will inevitably freak out, and they look to us to be that calm in the storm. For example, 9/11 was an unprecedented disruption for government and business. "There was no way to plan for something like that, it was very much like being in a storm at sea. We can't waste time in inaction, we focus on what we can control. We stay calm and keep going, doing the best we can, making the best decisions in the moment."

4. **Honesty.** A corollary to this is to be able to think long term. One of our most important assets is our reputation. It's important to be right, most of the time. If we're not honest, we can't have trust. When we have the most information, it's wasted unless we have the courage and confidence to be honest. Madigan admits that he's pissed off colleagues on more than a few occasions and even lost business in the

short term by sticking to his guns. However, he found it always paid dividends in the long-term, "especially when I was proved right." He smiles, with just a touch of ego.

5. **Optimism.** As consultants, our job is to find the solution and that requires energy and optimism. No one wants to work with pessimists or naysayers or to be told it can't be done. That's why we hire lawyers. This is not encouragement for delusion; as with everything, it requires balance.

He also points out that

TRUST WORKS BOTH WAYS

Some clients like to play the gotcha game. They look for every opportunity to prove us wrong, proving that they are as smart and even smarter than the consultant. It can be a signal that they don't trust us, don't value us, and want to keep us in our place. In general, we want to avoid those clients.

We want to have confidence in and trust our clients as much as they trust you. That's how we do our best work.

BOUNDARIES AND RESPECT

"Give respect, get respect."

—GEORGE NASUTI, COACH, HIGH SCHOOL
PRINCIPAL, AND MY UNCLE

I was discussing managing egos and flow in teams with one of my favorite people, Michelle Mahony, senior principal at

Daggerwing.[84] She reminded me "it may seem counterintuitive, but one of the best ways to earn trust with a new client is to know when to say no."

"It's sort of like that one guy you dated in college." She laughs a little at the metaphor. "The super nice guy, who never said no and let you walk all over him. It never worked out, no matter how nice he was, because you just couldn't respect him."

"Oh my god, how did you know?" I said. "I'm not going to lie, I'm pretty sure I've been on both sides of that relationship."

Not letting clients walk all over us is not about us or our ego. It's about creating trust and a partnership. Knowing the boundaries, and clarifying the scope is reassuring to clients. Not only are bully clients no fun to work with, they risk burning out our teams and generally produce worse results. They are not the experts, no matter what they think.

The client's needs come first, and they don't always know best—that's why they hire us as the expert. We, as the "expert," need to be an expert in at least two things. First, the subject matter, which is obvious, and second, how to listen and match our expertise with the client's needs.

WHO'S ENTITLED TO SELF-CONFIDENCE?

In the introduction to the Flow List, I touched on my own challenge moving past the bizarre consensus that I suddenly "lacked confidence." What I didn't say was that in my written

---

84 Michelle Mahony, Interview, 2019.

review, in addition to the feedback that I was a pushover, another director also wrote that I was *too* decisive. Specifically, he included that I had a "take it or leave it" attitude. It seemed I both lacked confidence and was too confident.

It hurt. After all that time busting my butt on scut work, trying to earn trust, it was textual data that I could no longer ignore—proof that all my efforts had been wasted.

However, it was also a gift.

In my efforts to learn to be more confident, I was becoming an expert on confidence, which gave me a whole new heuristic model, including an understanding about the language of exclusion. That, combined with over ten thousand hours analyzing big data sets including social commentary and extracts from surveys and HR systems, gave me a unique perspective.[85]

I was grateful to have the feedback in writing. It was tangible proof, at least to me, of the unconscious leadership assumptions and impossible situation I'd been experiencing for months.

Digging into data, interviewing, and now serving hundreds of other people, I realize that my experience was not unique.

---

85 From 2013 to 2016, I worked with my firm's proprietary social media data set, analyzing millions of global comments pulled from Twitter, Facebook, Quora, Reddit, Industry Discussion Boards, and dozens of other sources, analyzing commentary for sentiment and insights—helping major Automotive companies understand the impact of the marketing campaigns, competitive positioning and latent and unmet customer needs in emergent products like electric vehicles and self-driving cars.

Figuring out the "balance" between being appropriate and threatening is an all too common conundrum. Recalling Sallie Krawcheck's story, she was criticized for the hubris of being a public figure, implicitly accused of being egotistical when all she'd been doing was following orders.

When caught in this vortex, it may feel like we are

NEVER GOOD ENOUGH

Folks in this space feel like they are on constant high alert and in a state of constant reactivity. That feeling of "never enough" and constantly needing to prove ourselves is toxic and is a signal of a noninclusive environment. In such environments, success may even feel like failure.

Success and achieving goals are not enough for sustaining flow, in part because they lack the joy and support of a team. When we feel like an outsider, the jealousy, contempt, and rejection of not belonging weigh on us. If we are not conscious of this feeling, we might be tempted to just deal with it. Many people were taught that work just sucks. That's why it's called work after all. And yet it's not true.

I don't have an easy catch-all solution. Sometimes we have to accept some short-term paying of dues, sometimes we bide our time until we can change the rules, and sometimes we need to cut our losses and fund more awesome people to work with.

I can tell you unequivocally it's not egotistical to know our worth and to negotiate for it. It's not entitled to expect mutual trust. It's smart because it sets us, our team, and our organizations up for mutual success.

Also, in case I haven't said this enough, smart confident people aren't intimidated by other talented people. Awesome people have better things to do than put people down.

FROM "ME & YOU" TO "WE"

Deference as a means of showing loyalty is not always effective. In fact, it is counterproductive and disempowering for members of the out-group. Kowtowing and ignoring one party's needs over the other can create feelings of contempt and reinforce barriers. Maintaining the distinction between you and me, even when it's coming from a place of kindness, reinforces separation, in contrast to prioritizing shared and mutually beneficial goals.

FINDING AGREEMENT AS A SUSTAINABLE SOLUTION

I used to evaluate proof of concept projects, or POCs, pilot projects to test out new AI and machine learning capabilities with our clients. At any one time, hundreds of partners submitted requests for the use of our data scientists' time and resources.

Some partners felt like it was all about the bottom line, so that they could win the work and impress their clients.

It didn't take long for an interesting pattern to emerge. The projects where we did the best work weren't just automating tedious tasks, which, to be fair, I don't think the senior auditors or tax accountants found to be as horrifically boring as others did. Our best successes came from tackling interesting projects. For example, one project included designing a robust analytics engine to help the National Basketball Association (NBA) visualize and identify schedule options that took into account roughly a bazillion parameters from travel time, distance requirements, home and away requirements, and accommodations for the venue event calendar—and it also allowed teams and owners to have input on various iterations.

It was messy, sticky, and wicked hard. The team could not have been happier. It wasn't just about the money. The work, as well as the client, excited the team and provided a lot of long-term lessons.

Too often we defer decisions to those with status and rank, when we really should collaborate.

BIG FISH THINKING

Let's consider this simple scenario. For simplicity's sake you can think of the "big fish" or leader as Mr. Burns and his team as Smithers. Folks who get the Simpsons reference will understand my implicit bias.

Also, in this scenario, let's consider that projects valued below 40, identified by an (*), are boring, draining, and lead to burnout. Also, because time is limited, let's assume only three projects can be selected.

Knowing this, what should we prioritize?

	Stakeholder "Value"		
	Mr. Burns	Smithers	Combined
Project 1	100	10*	110
Project 2	95	60	155
Project 3	85	20*	105
Project 4	70	60	130
Project 5	70	30*	100
Project 6	50	50	100

Without factoring in Smithers's perspective, Mr. Burns would obviously choose projects 1, 2, and 3 for a total of 280 for Mr. Burns and 370 for the team, including two of the three projects that burn out poor Smithers. Not bad for the short term, but not great in the long term.

Shifting to a collaborative view results in projects 2, 4, and 6 being selected. Mr. Burns nets 215, less than before, but the team nets 385 and has the added benefit of being more sustainable.

Perhaps this approach seems obvious. From my experience after negotiating around partners who are incentivized to maximize revenue, this kind of thinking often takes a back seat to the drive for profit and status.

IT'S NOT ME. IT'S YOU.

Making sense of my experience of feeling bullied and burned out, I had to accept that it really wasn't about me. It was about them, their ego, their perspective, and their view that superseded all else.

Like Cinderella hustling to complete her chores before being promoted to the ball, I was never supposed to dance with the prince. There were always more chores, reasons, or some obstacle to keep me in my place.

Stuck trying to guess what others wanted, I was thinking about them as separate from me. I was the one who had accepted the subjugation, the idea that I have to prove myself, and that they could even judge me.

For a while there, I thought I was holding on for one last external validation so I could punch my ticket and leave.

For a time, I let this make me feel stuck. I started to struggle to show up confidently. I could feel their approbation weighing on me and I hated that it made their opinion right.

In retrospect, it is understandable that I *felt* insecure, uncertain, and unsafe. I *was* insecure, uncertain, and unsafe. Their elephants and unconscious minds were certain that I had no value and no worth. I was stuck in "fake it 'til you make it" mode.

This is just how the system worked. They put outliers and anyone who did not fit "in their place." It was normal. I wasn't special.

They wanted unquestioned loyalty, trust, and respect. No matter how hard I tried, I couldn't give them that because deep down, I didn't feel they deserved it, even if I couldn't consciously admit it.

I had pushed tenaciously myself so hard that I went past the limits of my integrity and, in the process, burned out.

LOOK FOR THE HELPERS

"Humility is not thinking less of yourself, but thinking of yourself less."

—C.S. LEWIS

These days, when I feel low and helpless, I pause, take a breath, and look for ways to help others. Thinking about others always makes me feel better. My friend, Bryanda, reminds me that when we support our community,

IT'S NOT CHARITY, IT'S SOLIDARITY

I'm writing this during the COVID-19 pandemic. It's mid-April 2020, and we can almost taste the fear, as our world faces massive uncertainty from health to economic concerns. Many of us feel our most fundamental needs are threatened.

At the same time, there is cause for hope and opportunities to rise to the occasion.

In the same way I learned to trust my unconscious spirit elephant after the 2017 shooting, this crisis reaffirms for me the power of deciding what I give my attention to. I can give my attention to worry and fear by staring at the constant stream of coronavirus updates, people selfishly refusing to social distance, or politicians who seem more concerned about power than service. Or I can devote my attention to what energizes me. I can choose to be inspired by the healthcare workers and the everyday kindness of strangers.

Even when we feel like we have nothing tangible to offer, we can find flow and create art, transfiguring our pain and those of others into lessons and light. This is what artists and creatives do, what we have always done.

Neil Gaiman puts this idea into words much better than I can:

When things get tough, this is what you should do. Make good art. I'm serious. Husband runs off with a politician? Make good art. Leg crushed and then eaten by mutated boa constrictor? Make good art. IRS on your trail? Make good art. Cat exploded? Make good art. Somebody on the Internet thinks what you do is stupid or evil or it's all been done before? Make good art. Probably things will work out somehow, and eventually time will take the sting away, but that doesn't matter. Do what only you do best. Make good art.

—NEIL GAIMAN[86]

And, as if I needed any more reminders, this appeared in my inbox recently:

Throughout history, we have endured many crises and persevered. Some of the world's greatest art was created during those times, and many examples, which testify to the endurance of the human spirit, are found within our walls.

—NATIONAL GALLERY OF ART,
MARCH 31, 2020 E-NEWSLETTER

---

86 Neil Gaiman, University of the Arts Keynote Address, 2012, May 17, 2012.

I share with you this odd bit of kismet because it demonstrates the connective power and magic of flow. When we open up to the full energetic potential of existence, we start to notice the signs that have been swirling around us all along. We can consider these as gentle reminders that everything is connected, more deeply than we are aware of.

We are all both separate and together, and that we all have the ability to learn how to fly, or float in the flow.

JUST BE AWESOME

Remember, it's not about me or you. It's about us. Keep looking for the win-win, keep looking for ways that serve everyone. When we operate from a place of mutual benefit, service, and connection, we are our most powerful and rarely lack confidence.

CHAPTER FIFTEEN

TIMELESS

"Time and space are modes by which we think and not conditions in which we live."

—ALBERT EINSTEIN

The shifting sense of time is probably one of the most commonly identified aspects of the flow experience. The reason for this time distortion is that our "rider," that newfangled part of our brain that is responsible for language and telling time, is so absorbed in an activity she's not paying attention to the clock.

Being in the flow is estimated to be five times more productive than not being in the flow, as well as more enjoyable and energizing. That means in a typical five-day workweek, one day spent in flow can be as impactful as an entire week not in the flow.

It's one reason why some companies allow employees to use up to 20 percent of their time on projects that engage them. Twenty percent is also the same percentage of time that the Mayo Clinic found was necessary for doctors and surgeons to reduce the probability of burnout.

FLOW TIME

Not all time is created equal. According to one story, when Einstein's Theory of Relativity went "viral," reporters started calling up his office, asking him for a simple explanation. The scientist is also credited with suggesting that if we can't explain a concept to a five-year-old, we don't understand it well enough. True to form, he gave the following simple explanation to his secretary to share.

According to Einstein, the relativity of time is very much like how when we talk to a pretty girl for an hour it feels like a minute and when we sit on a hot stove for a minute it feels like an hour.

Exhibit 15.1 According to Einstein, time really does fly when we're having fun.

Our experience of time shifts according to how we feel. This is probably not a surprise. We all know that time flies when you are having fun, and yet for whatever reason, management does not take this fundamental tenet into account.

For me, that loss of a sense of time is probably the biggest indicator that I'm in flow. It's definitely something I've noticed writing this book. The "downside" of flow is that we can get so lost in it we might miss meetings, calls, and even physical cues like the need to eat and use the bathroom. We're friends now—I can admit that, right?

Flow time is such a present and, frankly, a fantastic feeling. It feels magical. It's easy to believe that it just happens.

However, it's not magical; we can create it very intentionally. The right decisions, habits, and boundaries working together help us create that space.

PRODUCTIVITY HACKS AND MANAGING OUR TIME

WE DON'T *HAVE* TIME, WE *MAKE* TIME

When people find out I teach yoga, they often confess, "I wish I did more yoga" or "I wish I had more time to do yoga." For the record, I do this to nutritionists, rock climbers, Francophones, and really anyone who does something admirable I suck at.

I, like those that confess to me, am a big fat liar.

The truth is, when I really want to do something, I do it. I've never once said to a baker, oh I wish I ate more cake. Trust me, I make sure to eat plenty of cake.

If I want to do something, I make the time. If it serves a need or want, we do it. It really is that simple.

When we catch ourselves saying one thing but doing another, we send mixed signals to our body and create stress. Instead, let's practice honesty and be mindful of our language. Instead let's just say "that's cool, go on with your awesome self," or "I really admire that."

There is no need to fib, we can just explain we'll be too busy eating cake to go to Zumba. Totally understandable.

WHEN IT COMES TO PRODUCTIVITY, YOU ARE A UNIQUE SPECIAL UNICORN

Don't get a big head—everyone's a special unicorn. What that means is, like all the advice in this book, we have to experiment a little to find what works for us. There are a ton of productivity books about optimizing our time, not to mention infinite articles on the internet. Not all the hacks work for everyone and we can, ironically, waste a lot of time studying productivity.

Be mindful of the difference between knowing a tool and using it. It's like that unused treadmill or bread machine: it doesn't us do any good if we don't use it.

DO IT RIGHT, THE FIRST TIME

This is a lesson I learned early on from my dad. My dad worked in construction for roughly a hundred billion years. I tagged along, often enough to know that in construction, rushing has consequences in terms of quality costs and delays.

Measure twice, cut once. When we rush, we forget about the consequences rushing has.

- We don't have time to pay attention to our packing, so we have to take time to buy a new charger because we left ours at home.
- We don't have time to go to the doctor, but we have time to go to the hospital when we collapse at the airport.
- We don't have time to listen to our employees when they have issues, but we have time to interview and train new hires when good folks quit.
- We don't have time to develop a relationship with the client, but we have time to pitch ten times as many clients to win the same amount of work.

Be intentional about time and factor in long-term impact on short-term decisions. When unanticipated time drains come up, instead of getting annoyed, it helps to take a breath and get curious about the decisions and assumptions that led to the crisis. More often than not, there is some decision we overlooked or habit we missed that brought us to that crossroads.

TIME OF DAY

How we feel affects our decisions, and the time of day can have a surprising impact on not just our feelings but also how much energy our rider has to make decisions. Dan Pink's book *When* is an excellent primer on the topic. He discusses how understanding chronotypes—the best times of day according to our body's circadian rhythm—can help us structure our schedule by matching activities and decision-making with our energetic ebbs and flows.[87] The three established chronotypes include larks (aka early birds), owls (aka night owls), and third birds, the folks who are a combination of the two.

As an early bird, I do my best work as soon as I get up, generally around 6:00 a.m. until 11:00 a.m. After that, I experience a bit of a lull, which is a great time for me to recharge, doing easy tasks like editing, responding to emails, or listening to a podcast. I also schedule meetings where I don't need to create or make a lot of big decisions.

It may be helpful to experiment with our chronotype and observe our natural preferences to figure out what works for us.

DEAL WITH SHORT-TERM DISTRACTIONS FOR LONG-TERM RESULTS

Let's face it: we all get distracted. Even mindfulness and productivity coaches aren't perfect. Actually, we're probably the most flawed and imperfect. As an ideator, I get ideas all the time, way more ideas than I can explore. One of the things I'm pretty good at is prioritizing based on what I can finish. Generally, when an idea visits, I can gently put it on the shelf or write it down in my journal and get back to it later.

Still, in the middle of writing this book, I found myself called to create a course on managing burnout specifically for healthcare workers that I couldn't shake.

---

87   Daniel H. Pink, *When* (New York: Riverhead Books, New York, 2018), 27.

From the science of motivation, we know how short-term and extrinsic need goals can sideline long-term goals. I have a pretty good rapport with my elephant brain and I am generally able to convince her to work with me. She's pretty good at not buying shoes, eating gummy bears, or making out with cute people at parties after a few shots. In the case of this sideline project, none of the normal Jedi mind tricks were working.

So, I gave in, hustled, and launched my first video course in three days. Problem solved.

If we can't beat our elephant, ride her.

OUR INNER ALARM CLOCK

Whenever I have to get up super early for a flight or a meeting with India or Europe, I find it difficult to sleep very deeply. I seem to have an "inner alarm clock"—a mental subroutine, running in the background that I have difficulty turning off. I first noticed this when I lived in Brooklyn. With 7 a.m. alternate side street parking, it was like I had a low-grade alert lingering at the edge of my consciousness. This constant irritation made it difficult to sleep deeply. These days, whenever possible I like to "outsource" those kinds of mental drains. Automatic digital tools can replace some of these mental drains.

TOMATO CLOCKS AND SPRINTING

Knowledge work often requires chunks of time for folks to get into the groove. Some organizations and teams very intentionally align their schedules and encourage folks to schedule in large chunks of uninterrupted time for deep-focused work.

Respect and support these time boundaries by encouraging employees to block off their calendar. Help your team hold that time sacrosanct, but understand it is a process. Work as a team to understand the rules for interrupting that time and the consequences for crossing those boundaries.

GETTING INTO THE GROOVE WITH THE POMODORO METHOD
A popular technique for many is known as the Pomodoro method, traditionally four short sprints of twenty-five minutes each with a five-minute rest in between, although some people use even shorter sprints.[88] This is an especially popular method for writers. It's surprising how much we can get done in such a short focused amount of time. I like the Pomodoro method as a way to get my butt into the chair. It can also be effective as a facilitation tool for demonstrating the power of focused effort. It's especially useful when we're feeling overwhelmed or stuck in our head.

DONE IS BETTER THAN PERFECT
There is a saying that time often expands according to the task. An illustration of this idea is below. Sprints are good to focus on and set limits. Limitless time is actually overwhelming and may create anxiety.

---

88 Tucker Cummings, "Does the Pomodoro Technique Work for Your Productivity?" *Life Hacker*, April 14, 2020.

OCTOPUS DRAWINGS

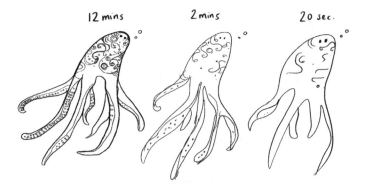

Exhibit 15.2 - The above illustration shows the varying level of quality depending on time. Sometimes it helps to clarify what is "good enough" when scoping work, since work often expands based on the amount of time we have.

One of my professors used to come into class about ten minutes before the end of every exam and announce, "eighty percent of what you needed to get down was in the first 20 percent of this exam." He had a point, although I suspect he also wanted to minimize having to read lengthy essay-like answers.

BEING IN THE PRESENT MOMENT

One thing I notice while working with overachievers is that they ping-pong between worrying about past problems and future anxieties.

They give off an almost frenetic and uncertain vibe. Stuck in their head and focused on how they think things *should* be, these overachievers can get so wrapped up in their vision they lose the moment and the opportunity to connect.

It's happened to many of us. We can get so caught up trying to impress someone in an interview, meeting, or pitch, and guessing at our client needs that we miss the opportunity to actually ask, listen, and discover client needs.

I used to assume I had to have all the answers. I call it West Wing syndrome, based on how Donna Moss, the ultra-capable assistant to Josh Lyman, anticipated his needs with an almost prescient foresight. She just knew everything.

She was also an imagined fabrication of Aaron Sorkin. In real life, people aren't semi-telepathic and don't talk that fast.

Take a deep breath. Slow down, get present, and listen more. Reflect back on what was said and confirm the shared understanding.

Honestly, if we did nothing else, this one piece of advice would change the world.

CAVEAT FLOW-EUR

One final thought about that experience of stepping outside time: one risk of pursuing timeless and effortless work is that unconscious managers may undervalue that work or take advantage of flow productivity and inadvertently block it.

For example, when bosses manage solely to the clock—butts must be in chairs from 8 a.m. until 5 p.m.—it is often a sign that the culture values conformity over autonomy and the appearance of work over actual results. Folks who find efficiency in the state of flow may wreck the curve for everyone else and be held in contempt by co-workers and even managers.

We have to be aware of power dynamics. Flow requires space to pulse and explore. Flow can be crushed in an unsafe, unsupportive, or mindless competitive environment.

Losing ourselves in flow may indeed be risky and even impossible if we need to be constantly on guard.

TL;DR

When we support our teams in creating time boundaries to creating and sustaining flow, not only do we get better results, we get happier employees. Unfortunately, relegating unpleasant, tedious, and boring tasks is one of the purposes of hierarchy. Managers and organizations that are unconsciously committed to false hierarchies and establishing status and power over others may rationalize refusals to allow people autonomy and flexibility over their schedule.

CHAPTER SIXTEEN

LOVE AND CARE

Writing about love and care in a business book makes me uncomfortable. Partly because many folks still believe acting like a human at work is a "nice to have." They feel like worrying about feelings and being nice is a distraction from doing the real work and getting results.

Let's face it—it's a bit obvious for a woman to be writing about this touchy-feeling crap.

"Love is the answer" is a total cliché. How many stories come down to the source of magic being love? Harry Potter, Sleeping Beauty, Practical Magic, Narnia, and so on. I expect if you are a serious businessperson, you are about ready to fling this book away in disgust.

I hear you. I wish I didn't have to explain this stuff either. From my perspective, this stuff is so basic on so many levels. I shouldn't have to explain it at all, but here we are. Here's the thing: those of you who just want to burn this book right now probably need this part the most. So, let's rip off the Band-Aid.

THE NAIVE BUSINESSPERSON

"Even the most hard-nosed performance-oriented organizations desperately want you to find great love in what you do... they just don't call it that."

—MARCUS BUCKINGHAM AND ASHLEY GOODALL, *NINE LIES ABOUT WORK*[89]

A lot of thought leaders, from Simon Sinek to Brené Brown to Marc Brackett, admit that they've been told at some point by a CEO or other leader that their views on belonging, love, feelings, and cooperative models are "naive." Some senior leaders push back on the importance of soft skills, things like cultivating trust, compassion, and consideration. Some folks just believe that the world is fundamentally a dark and selfish place. However, research also shows companies with a high level of trust, respect, and emotional safety perform the best. So respectfully, f*** those folks.

IT'S LOVE, OBVIOUSLY

"What is so extraordinary about the power of human connection is it's something that feels so simple, that we take for granted, it has this ability to heal in extraordinary ways.... there is nothing more powerful than love, in terms of its ability to heal."

—DR. VIVEK MURTHY, NINETEENTH US SURGEON GENERAL[90]

89 Marcus Buckingham and Ashley Goodall, *Nine Lies About Work* (Harvard Business Review Press, 2019).

90 Brené Brown, (host), "Dr. Vivek Murthy and Brené on Loneliness and Connection," *Unlocking Us*, April 21, 2020.

Let's break it down. We know that flow is the best feeling. Flow is that experience of being most energized and most alive. What else is the best feeling?

What do we loooooove?

Love, obviously.

Love is pure inspiration, spirit, source energy, and motivation. Love elevates us, opens us up and makes us feel brave and courageous.

Love transforms us. It makes the days better and is generative. Like Dumbledore says, love is the most powerful force on earth. Love is flow, and as we know, flow helps us be our most productive, innovative, creative, resilient, open, and powerful selves. In short, love is energy.

If you feel weird thinking about it as love, feel free to think about it as power, motivation, mojo, respect, verve, or drive. Whatever works for you.

LOVE IS RADICAL[91]

From eighth grade through sophomore year of high school, my mom insisted I study Latin as my foreign language. Ostensibly this was to help me on my SAT vocabulary, but really she just thought it was cool. Not gonna lie, I'm still a bit bitter. For the last thirty years, I've had first and second

---

91 Radical comes from the Latin word "rad" meaning "root," which is pretty gnarly when you think about it.

declensions, not to mention random Latin mottos, bouncing around my head.

On the bright side, I scored in the ninety-something percentile on my SATs. The bad news is, studying Latin messes with our mind by exposing the bones of our language and, by extension, the roots of our reality. It's from this perspective that I can't help but see how love is everywhere when we look and dig into the etymology.[92]

For example:

- Dig into "curiosity," and you'll find "cura" meaning "care," which makes sense because we are curious about things about which we *care*.
- Unpacking generosity, we notice that generous comes from the root of Genus, meaning "stock," or "noble lineage." So, we can infer that the *essence* of what is to be of human stock and noble is to generate, to create, and consequently to give to others.
- Examine the word courageous and we find at its heart "coeur," literally the French word for "heart." In addition to being brave, courage means to act from the heart, to live and work in one's convictions.
- When we do work from our convictions, we are whole, aligned and *integrated* and coming from a place of *integrity*. To be courageous is to also be integrated.

---

92 This may be a delusion and a result of cognitive bias or it may, in the words of Vladimir Nabokov, be a result of "Genius finding the invisible link between things," which definitely reeks of hubris and delusion, but bear with me.

- Speaking of hearts, the heart is a common symbol of love, and to be open-hearted and whole-hearted is to be generous, bold, powerful, and kind.
- "To matter" to someone also means to be cared about, which is to have substance, to be real and valid in this world, as opposed to the ephemeral substance of dreams and wishes.

Just looking at our words, what it means to be human is rooted in love and connection. It forms our unconscious understanding and assumptions about our very being.

LOVE AND WAR METAPHORS

"Vulnerability sounds like truth and feels like courage. Truth and courage aren't always comfortable, but they're never weakness."

—BRENÉ BROWN[93]

Somewhere along the way, as a society we've mixed up maturity and self-control with a lack of emotions, apathy, or repressing our emotions. We don't know how to distinguish the appearance of tranquility with the actual self-regulation of emotions.

Tennyson writes, "'tis better to have loved and lost, than never to have loved at all," but generations later, we prescribe away our feelings, preferring instead to not feel at all.

Expressing emotions, good or bad, is often considered vulnerable, weak, or needy.

---

93   Brené Brown, *Daring Greatly* (Penguin Random House Audio Publishing Group, 2017).

If we admit we care, some folks see that as a weakness to be exploited, believing that the person who cares the most in a relationship is at the greatest disadvantage. I'm not sure who to blame for this: Seinfeld, Queen Elizabeth II, or the 80s Wall Street culture that popularized the Art of War as a managerial playbook.

Consider one of the more famous quotes from Sun Tzu: "Appear strong when you are weak, and weak when you are strong." The fact that so many have bought into this culture of war and competition is disturbing. To paraphrase Sun Tzu, the Art of War is all about deception—the antithesis of trust. Given this bizarre, mixed-up approach to business, is it any wonder we are so upside down and backward in the way we lead and manage?

Many of us were raised to be competitive, exclusive, and not to trust. I was so good at competing I was a teaching assistant for competitive strategies. If I am being honest, I find old-school economics, as the study of fighting over limited resources, fascinating. Still, progressive companies are trending away from competitive and zero-sum old power models.

When we assume everything is a competition, we hyper focus, get tunnel vision, tighten, and exclude. We look to win as individuals and stop seeking ways to connect, share, and include.

When we are in competition mode, we may even argue there is no time or space for caring, love, trust, and humanity. When we are at war, we are not safe—we feel threatened and we protect ourselves and our heart. We build walls to protect and exclude others.

That feeling is how we know we are at war and how we know we are not safe. Even when war is our literal reality, there are still instances where we can benefit from trusting, to identify our allies, our comrades, or our teammates. We can connect and unify against a common enemy or toward a common purpose.

WHO HAS YOUR BACK?

I was talking about intentional culture creation with my friend Sherean Miller, managing partner at FMP Consulting, culture consultants for government agencies. Miller looks like what I imagine would happen if Ali McGraw had ever been a Charlie's Angel. This is partly because I usually see her kicking butt at 6 a.m. boot camp. Also, in addition to managing clients and operations for FMP, she's a certified Zumba instructor and a ray of sunshine.

One thing, I find most assuring about organizational consultants is that they generally practice what they preach.

She explained to me that when she and her two partners were initially negotiating to take over FMP, they began with a promise to each other.

"We knew it was a big opportunity and also a big risk [buying a controlling stake in the company]. Ultimately, it came down to trust. We promised each other that no matter what, we'd always have each other's back. It's been a cornerstone of our success, both among our leadership team and our organization."

When we work with folks who have our back, everything is easier. It's easier when we aren't distracted by people judging us, second guessing our ideas or motivations, or undermining our work. It seems obvious that when we are in a trusting relationship both the what and the how of the work is more awesome.

It's not crazy or naive to want or expect that.

DO OUR FEELINGS MATTER?

"The President doesn't like me, it is unambiguous... If you look at his Twitter account, you'll see my name quite often. None of it is good. It's hard to sit down and have a conversation with someone you have differences with and put that aside and say let's just do our jobs here... because it's bigger than we are. We're talking about life and death, the profound moment of our history. Let's just do it and forget everything else. And that's the way it should be, who cares how he feels, who cares how I feel about him personally. My feelings are irrelevant. My emotions are irrelevant. Just do the job."

—NEW YORK GOVERNOR, MARIO CUOMO[94]

One of the reasons why many folks believe emotions don't matter is that we are thinking in the short term. In a short-term crisis, we often need to put our feelings aside to get things done. This is normal and may very well be what we must do to survive.

Humbly, as much as I have appreciated the work Governor Cuomo has done, I disagree that in general and more broadly how we feel is irrelevant.

---

94 Daily Show with Trevor Noah, "Gov. Andrew Cuomo—Meeting Trump and Reopening New York | The Daily Social Distancing Show," *YouTube.*

As I mentioned, I used to bully and strong arm my unconscious elephant, using my short-term willpower to get things done all the time. It was how I was raised. I didn't know another way. Not knowing when to back down and how to honor my own boundaries left me burnt out, outside of my integrity, and disconnected from my heart and flow. Our emotions and understanding how to use them as data can help us prevent burnout. Emotions matter!

YOU WANT A CRISIS, I'LL GIVE YOU A CRISIS

It often feels like we are moving from one crisis to another. In reality, things are cyclical; life goes up and down.

In a pandemic crisis, we put those petty things aside. I suspect Cuomo's comment that feelings don't matter was more about the gossip twittering and petty sniping of other politicians.

Still, it's troubling, because out of context, without perspective, it sounds like our leaders are saying feelings don't matter, *ever*. We need to be a bit more mindful of our language and understand that our emotions matter *and* sometimes we still choose to set them aside.

In times of stress and crisis, we may have to combine forces to defeat a common enemy in the short term. Knowing when that term is over and pivoting is essential for long-term success. In the short term, we can push through and focus, repressing our feelings for a time. I have learned when it comes to emotions, there is always a reckoning.

Resent, coming from the French "sentir" and the suffix "re," meaning "to feel again."

It's` normal to pack away memory and emotion to deal with it later.

Unfortunately, when we unpack our emotions, boom, we feel that anger and frustration that we've bottled up. When we bury our feelings, they often pop up during times of stress precisely because we don't have the energy or strength to keep them locked up.

Think about your last argument with a family member. I don't know about you, but my family used to fight dirty. We'd bring up long forgotten grievances and old wounds. Failing to agree to a request could trigger an argument where the entire past comes up, from that Christmas in 1993 when we ate all the pecan pie, to that time we forgot to pick up Aunt Maggie at the airport, to leaving too much hair in the sink, to the ongoing debate of whether that scar on our brother was because he was clumsy and he tripped or because we pushed him. Or something like that... some details have been altered to protect the guilty.

We are all totally ridiculous and totally human. Disney got it right: we have to

LET IT GO
The way we do that begins with love. Forgiving those who hurt us but more importantly forgiving ourselves for being hurt, disappointed, and angry. Clearing space so that we

can also forgive those closest to our heart for hurting and disappointing us. Trusting others begins with understanding, loving, and trusting ourselves. We need each other.

Our elephant defaults to focusing on failures and disappointments, but our rider can train it to also notice joy and love.

When we trust that an intention may be good, when the execution comes up short, we can maintain the relationships, connection, and trust and grow our confidence. Instead of assuming that failures reflect a breach of trust, we can use it as a data point in our practice, an error to acknowledge and fix, and motivation to try again and get it right.

"DON'T CARE SO MUCH"
One piece of advice I've been seeing pop up in coaching circles a lot lately is to stop caring so much and stop trying so hard.

This may be the right advice in zero-sum situations where we won't be rewarded or recognized for the effort. In general, I'm pro over-delivering, but not if it's not needed or wanted, and not if it's going to be taken for granted or earn us the enmity of overly competitive colleagues.

It's fine to care, to go above and beyond, if it sets us up for success or creates opportunities. Unfortunately, sometimes we have bosses like the one Larry Page faced early in his career. Recognizing we have bizarro-brained bosses is unfortunate, but it beats sticking our head in the sand.

It's tempting to linger on justifiable feelings of disappointment, frustration, and anger but ultimately, those feelings are a waste of time. The sooner we can move through them and let them go, the sooner we can use our energy to focus on something better.

Looking back on my experience with burnout, I definitely cared way too much about the integrity of what I was doing, about the quality of my work, about my team, and about my company. I thought I was doing the right thing. The company motto was "do the right thing in the right way." To me, that meant following the golden rule and doing my best by collaborating, being a team player, and being open to proving myself.

That's all well and good when everyone else is acting the same way.

I failed to switch my behavior when it changed from collaboration to competition. To be fair to myself, what was communicated wasn't in line with how leadership acted. I was working remotely and wasn't able to pick up on the nonverbal cues that would have told me I was no longer safe.

I was trained to give 100 percent and to treat others like I wanted to be treated. That strategy worked pretty well but it was built on an assumption—an assumption that I was working in a reciprocal environment, that work would be recognized and rewarded, not resented and held against me.

ALL'S FAIR

One of my biggest takeaways is learning to trust our intuitive sense of whether we are in an atmosphere of trust, if we have enough peace and security to invest and grow or if we need to be on guard. Most of us are somewhere in between. Life is a dance, and we must learn when to trust, when to open and grow, and when to close off and defend ourselves. It's a balance between surviving and thriving.

> "Always assume good intentions."
>
> —INDRA NOOYI[95]

When we are committed to a relationship, we give other people the benefit of the doubt. We may not agree with them, but we trust they are coming from a place of sincerity and integrity, even when they are acting like total boneheads.

We may not agree or always like our teammates, but when we are on a team we can always find a reason to trust and respect them. We can distinguish between anger, which is love motivated by injustice, with hate and contempt.

When trust falls apart, we often feel like the other person is motivated by hate, not love. We may even assume they are self-centered and against us. We lose connection and we tense up, tighten up, doubt and second guess everything

---

95   Indra Nooyi, "The Best Advice I Ever Got," *Fortune*, 2008.

they do. We may even stop thinking of them as people and start thinking of them as the enemy.

This is not cool.

Without love, trust, and connection, relationships fail, teams fall apart, and cultures evaporate. Fortunately, we can change this—starting with ourselves.

III

THE PRACTICE

CHAPTER SEVENTEEN

AN UNEXPECTED OUTCOME

———

"We don't sit in meditation to become good meditators. We sit in meditation so that we'll be more awake in our lives."
—PEMA CHODRON[96]

What I "discovered" the day of the shooting was something that meditators have known for centuries. I discovered the power of opening up and surrendering.

At the risk of being overly precious about the experience, it taught me self-compassion.

This was not a lesson that came easily to me. I enjoy getting gritty. In case you can't tell, I love the part of me that is annoyingly stubborn. "Self-compassion" kind of sounds like bullsh*t (please don't tell other coaches I said that because as

———

96 Pema Chodron, *When Things Fall Apart* (Boston: Shambhala, 2016).

nice as they are, I'm sure they'd kick my butt for admitting that). "Self-compassion" sounds like what slackers do to let themselves off the hook.

Also, I should note that all my life, people have told me that I'm way too hard on myself. I didn't believe them. I'm not going to lie—I may have also secretly judged them for being way too nice.

I didn't want to go easier on myself, I had standards to uphold.

GETTING OVER MYSELF

I joke about it now, but don't let me fool you—that girl is still in here. I'm not sure I will ever lose her. I'm not sure I want to. I love that knuckleheaded inner skeptic. Meditation has helped me connect and trust my whole self; and helped me learn when to go easier on myself, just not too easy.

I recommend and teach meditation as a path to metacognition because it works for me. Other people have found this same kind of awareness in communities of faith, walking in the forest, practicing a sport or martial art, and even on the golf course. Many of us have a compulsion to proselytize what mindfulness habit worked for us. I believe everyone can become more aware. However, I also believe strongly that we need to find what works for us. I don't believe there is only one way to find connection and mindfulness.

I like meditation and breathing because it's accessible and cheap. I also lean introverted, so belly button gazing is kind of my jam.

ACTING IN NEW WAYS?

"The definition of insanity is doing the same thing over and over again and expecting a different result."

I often miss opportunities to use my newfound superpowers. Still, when it works it can be amazing. The first time, I was able to turn around a volatile situation in real time blew my mind.

THAT'S WHY THEY CALL THEM BUMPERS

First, I should warn you. This story is about an issue that is more divisive than many of our political beliefs. You may lose total respect for me. My friend Tracy Rabuse once commented that the way I behaved in this story would get me arrested in Georgia. I have no doubt she is right.

The world is divided between those people who think it is *occasionally* okay to gently tap bumpers when parallel parking and those who feel bumper tappers should be burned at the stake.

I am in the first category. I hope we can still be friends.

In my defense, I was raised believing bumpers were meant to be bumped, an attitude that was reinforced living in Manhattan, Brooklyn, and Philadelphia. Sometimes on very crowded streets, especially with alternate side street parking, we have to get a bit *assertive* with finding a spot. I'm sure Taylor Swift would agree, bumpers gonna bump.

AN UNEXPECTED OUTCOME · 205

With that in mind, imagine this scene: it's a bright spring day and I'm late to a meeting in downtown Washington, DC. I'd been circling for ten minutes when I see a bright blue Hyundai pull out in front of my destination. Whispering a quick thank you to the parking fairy, I pull up. I could already tell it would be tight, but I was in it to win it.

And it was tight, like really tight. Dammit, I was off my game.

I'd borrowed my brother's old Saturn for the day since my own car was in the shop. His car is a bit longer than my Altima, which, somehow, I forgot. It also doesn't have a rearview camera, which is totally a luxury, I'll admit, and one I'd become too reliant upon. That was how I found myself wedged in tight, inching back and forth at a glacial speed. I was in, but it wasn't pretty.

I had *maybe* six inches of space, total, front and back.

I'll admit, if I'd known the owner of the shiny black BMW I was trying to park in front of was sitting at the cafe across the street watching me eke back and forth, I would have definitely driven around the block.

This was even before I knew he'd come charging at me, screaming,

"WHAT THE F**K IS WRONG WITH YOU?"
That was my first clue he was in the second category.

"What kind of idiot are you? How could you think you could fit into that space? How stupid can you be?" His tirade went on for ten minutes. I'd thought I was stuck before, but there was no way I could leave now. Based on the bright red hue of his face, there was a real possibility that he might smash in my brother's windshield—or me.

There was not much I could do, so I took a breath. I had just subbed in two yoga classes for a friend and amazingly was still rocking some of that yoga bliss.

Also, it was broad daylight and my best guess was that he wasn't going to assault me, despite his repeated refrain that he was so angry he could "f**king punch me."

I did shift slightly on my toes noting a store nearby. On the upside, if he had a BMW, he probably had money, so I could sue, assuming he didn't kill me. Otherwise there wasn't anything I could do but listen.

So, I did.

That was when something interesting happened.

As he continue to yell, I started to imagine him sitting with his friends at the cafe as a beat up old Saturn tap-tap-tapped his bright shiny new BMW.

I could imagine his friends teasing him as he grew increasingly aggravated at the category one jerk who was probably wrecking his paint job.

While I was confident I hadn't done any damage, BMWs are fancy German machines and even small repairs would be expensive. I imagined a tiny scratch would cost a bajillion dollars. I tried not to think about that. Instead, I took a breath and let go of that thought.

One thing at a time, like not getting punched in public.

As respectfully as I could, I asked if he could perhaps back up so I could leave without risking touching his car again. I thought this request was rational and even considerate.

That was not how it was received. As hard as it was to believe, I actually pissed him off more and he continued to scream for several more minutes… and then finally, he paused and took a deep breath.

What he said next blew my mind.

"I know it's just a car. It's not worth freaking out over." WTF? Had I heard that right? Then he said the thing that broke my heart wide open.

"I'm sorry. I'm going through a lot right now." OMFG! I could relate to that. I'd been there. I'd been the hothead who cared too much so many times in my life. In that moment, I knew I could give him the understanding I'd always wanted from others when I overwhelmed them with my intensity.

"I get it," I said, and I meant it. I ignored my safe driver training and did what insurance companies tell you NOT to do: I apologized, sincerely. Then suggested we look at the bumper together. To be clear, this was not entirely altruistic; I wanted to get clarity on any damage for which I might be responsible and I wanted to do it before he went off on me again.

That was when he told me that he had just gotten the bumper specially painted. I felt another surge of empathy. He wasn't just a rich jerk; his car was his baby. I told him I could imagine how frustrating it was watching me park, and he laughed.

"I know it's just stuff," he said again, which allowed me to say, "it's a really nice paint job, I get why you'd worry." We both looked at it. To my relief, as well as his, there really was no damage.

We ended this encounter with a hug. Seriously, we hugged! I'll admit I'm a hugger and I regularly make people go in for the full twenty seconds, but even I was amazed by this turn of events.

When I returned a few hours later, to my immense relief, I saw that he'd pulled back several inches, which was enough for me to get out.

THE PAUSE IN PRACTICE

Sometimes, people just need to be heard and treated with respect. If we can, let them vent their fire, be patient and allow them to join us in the pause.

This turn around came because I was able to remain in the pause, to stay open and hold space for my own feelings as well as his. The forced silence was an opportunity to reflect, listen, and empathize. Holding the space long enough allowed BMW guy to eventually open up and join me. In that space we were able to talk and connect, and in the process, we let go of our emotions, our fears, and the stories we'd made up about the other person. If I had closed up, run away, yelled at or threatened him, things would have gone very differently.

Facing it at the time was scary, but looking back it taught me the power of listening and empathizing.

CHAPTER EIGHTEEN

THE TROUBLE WITH ASSUMPTIONS

"When you Assume, you make an Ass out of U and Me."

—POSTER ABOVE THE BLACKBOARD IN
MARY LOU WOODS'S BIOLOGY CLASS

CONVERSATION WITH A THOUGHT LEADER

While researching this book, I scored an interview with an influential creativity thought leader and entrepreneur I admired. After weeks of back and forth, I was excited to finally connect. Then, five minutes into the call, it went off the rails.

"That's kind of obvious," he said after I told him about the Flow List. Those words hit me like a punch to the gut. Awesome.

If he'd made that comment at the end of the call, I might have mumbled my thanks and hung up, but I didn't want to waste the meeting. So, even though I felt like a total loser, I took a deep breath and tried to stay curious.

"All those things are a no-brainer," he went on, before telling me about how in his start-up he already incorporates all the elements of the Flow List.

I was happy to hear an executive leading with clarity, feedback, and actively working to create environments where his team can focus and work without distractions. It's a sign of an empathetic style of leadership emerging with younger generations.

I learned that he himself had experienced burnout in the past. Although I sensed it was a topic he didn't want to talk about, it was clear that the experience had left a mark. I suspected, like Larry Page from the introduction, that experience informed the way he leads and taught him both empathy and perspective.

Unsurprisingly, we found a lot of common ground and yet I was stuck on his "obvious" comment.

Was it my ego? Was I just scared that I was going to have to scrap all my research? Worse, was I really unoriginal, even boring? We didn't disagree about the ideas, we disagreed about whether it was an insight and whether there was any value in writing about it. Had I spent months researching and talking to all those people for nothing?

After all, I had found in recent publications more evidence that these ideas were taking root. I'd just seen an illustration in *No Hard Feelings* making the connection between flow and burnout. These ideas were certainly obvious to me.

SIDEBAR

Let me take a step back and tell you something about me that is pretty true of working-class folks. I don't often think "I'm so smart." Just as stupid is as stupid does, smart is as smart does. Also, the psychological perks of being humble is that we remain curious and open… and behaving like a know-it-all is kind of obnoxious.

Still, there have been times that it has been useful to remind myself that I am smart. If something is not clear to me, it's often pretty hard for most people to get.

And then I realized:

THAT'S THE POINT!

The Flow List absolutely *should* be obvious to everyone! All this probably would have been obvious to me in my twenties, but somehow it got obscured by corporate bullsh*t. Like Odom's story from Chapter Three, my experience had left me cynical and jaded, corroding my faith in human entitlements.

The Flow List should be taken for granted by everyone. The fact that the principles are not always accessible or universally offered is a huge blind spot for leaders. No one should have to fight for the things on the Flow List. The fact that some of us have to negotiate and even beg for them while others are just handed them is a big part of the problem.

All the things in the Flow List are taken for granted by the in-group—the folks at the top, the folks for whom the system and our default biases defer.

People should always be given clarity, feedback, and appropriate levels of autonomy to do their job, free from interference, and tasks that fairly match their skills and strengths.

High-status people assume most of these things unconsciously, without question.

WHAT'S HOLDING YOU BACK?

Many people, mostly men but women too, many of whom I like and respect and who I look to as mentors and advisors, "don't get it."

They don't understand why I have been so tenacious at clarifying these unspoken assumptions. They don't get why everyone doesn't just assume this level of entitlement. They assume it's a personality thing, possibly a lack of confidence, will, or energy. Many coaches and mentors automatically push creatives and entrepreneurs to "just do it."

I don't entirely disagree, but I also see the other side.

While most folks can be taking more risks, I also think a lot of mentors and coaches advise mentees to do what worked for them. They tell folks to leap and the net will appear—without a full understanding of their mentee's context. They don't fully understand the risks holding folks back, especially how they are exacerbated by biases and systemic inequities that those they mentor may face.

This is dangerous. These coaches have no skin in the game and are not accountable. They don't understand how bias increases both actual and perceived risk. They don't understand how debt and bullying demoralize and how just *feeling* like low status, "low potential," decreases folks' opportunity. All these extra difficulties, delays, and struggles are an energy drain and function like a double and even triple whammy.

Our experience, our feelings, are not just in our head; they are in our body, and they matter. We thrive when we have a community that understands and respects our elephant's intuition and assumption, and we struggle when our community doesn't get it, doesn't believe, or doesn't trust that intuition.

"THAT HASN'T BEEN MY EXPERIENCE"

I've heard some form of that comment many, many times, mostly from middle-class white folks who are focused on raising their family and paying their bills. No disrespect—we all need to pay our bills.

These days, that phrase most often comes up when I speak about barriers to inclusion. Hearing this line was especially painful when I was trying to make sense of my experience of burnout, exclusion, and what felt like bullying.

As I shared my experience, I could see the thoughts flit across the faces of my friends. I could almost see the gears in their heads grinding as they tried to make sense of my story.

I was asking them to reconcile my experience with their faith in the system. It was a big ask. The process had worked for them, so their assumption was that I must be wrong, I must be mistaken, that burnout and bias was a result of my lack of grit, or worse, an unseen sense of entitlement or some other personality defect.

CHECK YOUR ASSUMPTIONS

My natural inclination was to accept the game at face value and accept the challenge to prove myself.

After years playing the game, I had to step back. When I tried to collect on dues paid, reminding my bosses of my track record, I found that no one but me had been keeping score. The game and the rules had changed when I was busy grinding away.

We don't always know who gets a free pass. We don't always recognize when some people are viewed as more credible "just because," while others have to work extra hard to be heard.

Like other women of my generation, I didn't realize that I would be underestimated my entire life or what impact that would have on my earning potential. Studying civil rights as a part of history, I didn't realize that many leaders in the present had no interest in changing their assumptions.

I found people insisting and rationalizing that the system worked because it worked for them. The lack of empathy and understanding made me feel even more alone, ashamed, and disconnected. If I was really so great, how could my company ignore me?

I struggled to makes sense of it.

Again, that is the point. No one is so good, so brilliant, so awesome that they can't be ignored, or excluded, if the folks in power are determined to do so. Being gritty isn't enough. One thing I noticed was that people with status, money, and better support systems than I had deal with bullying by quitting.

They find better games, better people, better situations. In short, they don't tolerate BS.

Like many folks from a working class background with staggering student loan debt, I didn't feel like this was an option. I was also raised to be gritty and stubbornly stoic. My folks were good at suffering and proving themselves—who was I to think I was any better?

Taking a step back, I realized that suffering is for chumps and martyrdom is boring. I also realized I wasn't alone. Many folks find themself similarly stuck. We get stuck on this treadmill because the upper-middle class elites keep moving the goal post.

Coaches can preach about mindfulness and focusing on what we can control. I'm all for changing the stuff we can, but let's not delude ourselves. The system is rigged.

IF IT'S BROKE, FIX IT
"Systems are perfectly designed for the results they get." My friend and wise woman Lynn Borton, host of the radio show Choose to Be Curious, once reminded me.

She learned this truism from her time as the Chief Operating Officer of the National Alliance on Mental Illness. We were discussing women in leadership and the double-edged sword of having a degree from Yale and the frustrating lack of progress in equality over the last twenty years.

There are plenty of articles that point out that "success" in one's job is not related to IQ, talent, ability, degrees, qualifications, or even hard work. Looking at the data, it seems that what makes folks rise in their career is ineffable and impossible to pin down. Some could argue that it has as much to do with luck and timing as anything else.

What a lot of articles seem to miss is the obvious. Success seems to be most strongly correlated with being rich, male, cis, straight, "white," able-bodied, married, and entitled—at least in America.

NOTHING BREEDS SUCCESS LIKE SUCCESS
Being overqualified, over-credentialed, and underemployed is correlated with being a part of a group that is marginalized, underrepresented, and disempowered.

What this means systemically is that we're failing to match talent with opportunity and in the process, we're failing our people and our economy.

Mindless leaders give the benefit of the doubt to the in-group, people in the same social status or higher. People who are outsiders are held to higher standards and are expected to have already proven themselves in their role, rather than given the opportunity to grow into it.

These leaders unconsciously believe that *their* path is the way to succeed.

They don't question whether their success had to do with accurate decision-making or luck. They believe that their success was entirely result of talent, work, and effort. What many fail to recognize is the role luck, timing, and even bias play regarding factors like access to opportunities, promotions, sponsorship, and encouragement.

RESULTING: SEPARATING GOOD DECISIONS FROM LUCK

I came across the idea of "resulting" from Annie Duke's book *Thinking in Bets*, which is based on her experience as both a psychologist and professional poker champion. Resulting is when we confuse a good outcome with a good decision.[97]

	Bad Decision	Good Decision
Good Result	You Got Lucky—Appreciate it but Don't Do It Again.	Keep Doing! (Obviously)
Bad Result	Stop Doing. (Obviously)	Unlucky—Keep at it.

My favorite example of resulting in practice is from Alex Honnold.[98] Honnold is famous for soloing El Capitan, which was documented in the movie *Free Solo*.

---

97 Annie Duke, *Thinking in Bets* (New York: Portfolio, 2019.)
98 Alex Honnold "How I Climbed a 3,000-Foot Vertical Cliff—Without Ropes," *TED*, April 2018.

Listening to Honnold talk about his experience climbing Half Dome during his TED Talk, we'd think that as a free solo climber he'd be super risk-seeking. In fact, he would say he is the opposite. He is just really good at meticulously removing risk. In particular, I love his clear-eyed reflection on when he failed to do that during his climb at Half Dome.

> "Between me and the summit lay a blank slab of granite... I had to trust my life to the friction between my climbing shoes and the smooth granite. I reached a foothold I didn't quite trust... I started to panic. I knew what I had to do but I was too afraid to do it. I just had to stand up on my right foot. And so after what felt like an eternity, I accepted what I had to do..."

—ALEXANDER HONNOLD

After surviving that risky maneuver just before summiting, he knew he "had gotten away with something. I didn't want to be a lucky climber. I wanted to be a great climber... I knew that I shouldn't make a habit of relying on luck."

What he is talking about is his refusal to buy into "resulting."

He knew better.

Most of us don't face life or death consequences with each decision we make. We don't need to be so introspective, but maybe we could benefit from a bit more curiosity.

BIAS AND LUCK

"I think it is some degree of hard work, for sure. There's also some degree of luck… By luck, I mean that I never worked for a Charlie Rose or a Matt Lauer or tried to make a movie with a Harvey Weinstein. Also, I never worked for a Todd. Who's Todd? Todd is that middle manager who's so terrific and nice and has a daughter and talks about unconscious-bias training classes but, still, he just never promotes a woman. Some of the women in my business school class got caught working for predators, but more of them got caught working for a Todd. It's just luck that I didn't."

—SALLIE KRAWCHECK[99]

Bias and luck may seem similar. I'm not sure we can tell them apart on the ground, when it's just one data point. It's really only in the aggregate that we can see the bigger perspective. It's easy to rationalize our decisions without context.

---

99 Charlotte Cowles, "The Motivating Power of Staying Pissed Off," *The Cut*, October 23, 2019.

When we zoom out, we notice only 20 percent of leadership is female. That means that men are four times more likely to be leaders at any given time. This is not luck; this is bias.

	Bad Decision	Good Decision
Good Result	Lucky Overvalued	Assumption
Bad Result	Stop Doing (Obviously)	Unlucky Marginalized Disbelieved Undervalued

LUCK IS WHEN OPPORTUNITY MEETS PREPARATION

We are taught that success requires hard work. It also requires luck. Some luck includes events outside of our control. Bias affects access to opportunities in ways that are both subtle and not subtle. Growing our skills and establishing credibility requires the opportunity to practice deliberately and get feedback. We can't grow and find flow if we don't have the chance to practice.

THE ATOMIC POWER OF LITTLE SHIFTS

James Clear has an excellent illustration of the benefits of incremental shifts, which I appreciate and is included below. In his book *Atomic Habits,* he doesn't often focus on the 1 percent decline line. That second line illustrates how little negative shifts make a good person gradually grind down. To me, it looks depressingly similar to burnout.[100]

---

100 James Clear, *Atomic Habits* (New York: Avery, 2018).

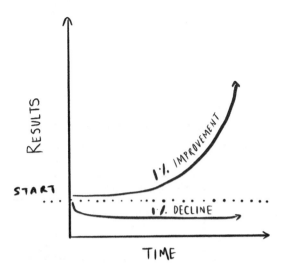

Exhibit 18.1 - Recreated from *Atomic Habits* by James Clear

Consider how a 1 percent bit of discouragement, noninclusion, avoidance, lack of trust, or lack of understanding would make us feel. All those little assumptions and microaggressions build up like poison. When a high-status person asks for clarity, it's assumed the assignment was unclear and they are given what they need without question. When a low-status outsider makes the same request, they are judged as needy, annoying, and entitled. Make no mistake—people can feel when we are thrown shade. Judgment destroys trust.

Our emotions, right or wrong, often color and determine our perspective. Studies have found that when teachers grade papers in a bad mood, the average scores go down.

Many of us have experienced shade and negative assumptions. When we pick a fight with our partner, anything they say can be taken the wrong way. One friend hated a female politician I supported. I told her that based on what I saw there was no way the politician could be indicted of a crime. My friend responded that either she's guilty or it just shows how corrupt the system is.

In other words, my friend had already made up her mind. Facts did not matter.

	Not Found Guilty	Found Guilty
She Is Guilty	Just Shows How Corrupt the System Is	The Right Outcome
~~She Is Not Guilty~~	Not Possible	Not Possible

We can feel when people are hoping that we fail. It's called "throwing shade," and it sucks. We don't have to like other people, but we do have to treat everyone with respect and dignity.

THE EMOTIONAL PATH OF SUCCESS

SPARTANS AND THE FAST TRACK

A lot of "successful" people are overrated at first. That's good for them because they get access to opportunities and challenges to set them up for success. This suits the Spartan emotional shape.

This leaves a huge opportunity for underrated underdogs. Spartan leadership doesn't always understand the value of Minervas or Gardeners, how they act or their signals.

Consider this example from Brené Brown's research:

"We asked a thousand leaders to list... what do your team members do that earns your trust? The most common answer: asking for help. When it comes to people who do not habitually ask for help, the leaders we polled explained that they would not delegate important work to them because the leaders did not trust that they would raise their hands and ask for help." [101]

Spartan leaders may assume that they employ Firecrackers, who push their limits and expect support. There is an unwritten expectation that we ask for help, but what about the folks who don't need it?

I'm thinking about Gardeners and Minerva types that often don't need help since their skills often exceed the challenge. Unfortunately, not asking for help may send the wrong signal to their leaders.

Another reason Gardeners and Minervas don't ask Spartans and Firecrackers for help is because sometimes, they are not as skilled or competent, are unreliable, or otherwise act like takers. Communicating dissatisfaction with a high-status player's quality of work is also problematic when we layer in the social expectations that low-status people must also be extra agreeable and must never be seen as strident or angry.

---

101 Brené Brown, *Dare to Lead* (New York: Random House, 2018), 219.

In this way, over-skilled, underemployed, and underrated folks can get stuck as unrecognized and overqualified leverage. Such habitual cycles, if not corrected, lead to attrition, frustration, and burnout.

The biggest leaps and amplifications come when we collaborate and trust, but to do that we need to clarify our assumptions and be explicit and accountable for the skills we are measuring, encouraging, and promoting.

LEAPING TO CONCLUSIONS

While most of us have been trained to hustle, it is often effective to take time at the beginning of the process and clarify assumptions. Be aware of what is happening below the conscious surface and take the time to unpack problematic habits when they emerge.

When people don't act like we expect, we are often better served by sitting down and having a conversation than by doubting them. Get curious, start with trust, and assume respect. Sometimes we have to solve these human issues before we get to the "real work."

For leaders, this is in fact "the real work."

CHAPTER NINETEEN

THE POWER OF PARADOX

———

Paradox is when something is true but appears to be contradictory. I think the reason we like dichotomies, those "either-or" binary choices, is because they are just easier to grasp. Being contradictory or contrary often has a negative connotation. It can be felt to be disagreeable, uncomfortable, and unpleasant, especially when uttered by someone of lower status. I hope we're beginning to appreciate the power in this friction, the power in conflict and in oppositional forces working in tandem. Sometimes conflict—two sides working against each other—is what we need to find balance.

DON'T STAY IN YOUR LANE

I believe these cops are intentionally trying to inflame the situation. They want an excuse.
@IBBN: "Music... Stay In your lane"
@Legend: "Human. Citizen. Taxpayer. I'm in my lane homie."[102]

—JOHN LEGEND, @JOHNLEGEND

———

102 John Legend (@johnlegend). *Twitter* August 14, 2014, 12:14 a.m.

In my opinion, Chrissy Teigen's amazingly talented husband, John Legend, had the perfect rebuttal to an attempt to put him in his place.

Artists, writers, and creatives wear many hats. Creativity is about making novel connections, connecting ideas, people, experiences, information, and data, and transforming them into something new, universal, and hopefully super cool.

A creative's ability to shift between heuristic models (e.g., thinking like a businessperson, artist, scientist, or engineer), perspectives (e.g., leaders, followers, clients), experiences, cultures, and so on can make them hard to pin down and difficult to understand. They are, in a word,

WEIRD

I get it. Between you and me, every time an actor launches an album or a singer gets into acting, I'm irrationally irritated. In my defense, for every Hailee Steinfeld or Leslie Odom, Jr., there's a Britney Spears or Madonna. Justin Timberlake took a while to grow on me, but he got better, which goes to show what practice can do.

Please note: If anyone says anything bad about Jennifer Hudson or Mandy Moore, they're dead to me. Seriously though, that's a little weird, right? I'm not sure which cognitive bias that is—let's call it my lazy jerk bias. Our need to pigeonhole folks is lazy and lacks imagination. Unfortunately, we do it all the time, creating false choices when we don't need to.

BEWARE FALSE DICHOTOMIES

Social scientists are taught to watch out for "false dichotomies," when an idea is presented as an either-or proposition. When presented with a choice, it helps to question whether it's truly binary and at the same time to ask who benefits from forcing such a choice.

Many women feel a false dichotomy when they are forced to choose between being liked or seen as competent.[103] Many kinds of false dichotomies exists, such as when low-status people feel like they have to choose between job security or speaking from a place of integrity, when men must choose between appearing strong or expressing vulnerability or emotions, and when spiritual icons are expected to be zen and not even a little funny.

At the heart of these apparent dichotomies are correlations and norms. If we want, we can unpack them with an X-Box analysis!

As a reminder, below is a generic X-Box breakdown.

	Characteristic B— Low	Characteristic B— High
Characteristic A— High	Outlier—"Weird"	Correlated— "Normal"
Characteristic A— Low	Correlated— "Normal"	Outlier—"Weird"

---

103 Marianne Cooper, "For Women Leaders, Likability and Success Hardly Go Hand-in-Hand," *Harvard Business Review*, April 30, 2013.

We can apply a super simplified X-Box analysis around gender and characteristics.[104]

	Demure /Passive	Assertive/ Aggressive
Male	Mostly Untrue— "Weird"	Mostly True— "Normal"
Female	Mostly True— "Normal"	Mostly Untrue— "Weird"

We all want to feel understood, and that impulse can often keep us in our place. The impulse to be accepted, understood, and liked can keep us trapped and block us from embracing balance and owning our full potential. Not only do we seem to be moving toward a more nuanced way of being, research suggests that people who exist in these liminal, grey areas may be more creative.

PSYCHOLOGICAL ANDROGYNY

In a 2017 lecture on creativity, Professor Richard Foster describes creative folks as "psychologically androgynous."[105] He explains how creatives often don't fit easily into either-or dichotomies and embrace the paradox of being both and finding their balance between extremes.

---

104 I wish it went without saying, but I realize that including only binary genders is a simplification. Non-binary gender exclusion from the "normal" is something I am hoping to increase both in my own and our collective awareness around. This simplification also illustrates the point that "either-or" choices often feel easier to understand than "both-and" or even "neither-nor."

105 Richard Foster, "Prof. Richard Foster on Creativity," *Yale School of Management,* YouTube.

According to Foster, these folks are "both extroverted and introverted, aggressive and nurturing, sensitive and rigid, dominant and submissive, conservative yet risk-seeking, humble yet proud and have a sense of sunny pessimism."[106] These opposing traits allow such creatives to find previously unassociated ideas and fields and, in the process, substantially improve their output.

BALANCED DICHOTOMY EXAMPLES

"The mark of a wild heart is living out the paradox of love in our lives. It's the ability to be tough and tender, excited and scared, brave and afraid—all in the same moment. It's showing up in our vulnerability and our courage, being both fierce and kind."

—BRENÉ BROWN[107]

Since coming across this research on creative paradox, I keep noticing examples of the energetic power of balancing between oppositional forces.

For example:

1. In meditation, we come to a posture of "relaxed alertness."
2. Two of our most basic human needs are "certainty" and "novelty."
3. As humans evolved, they developed a taste and appreciation for neophilia, the desire to try new things, and neophobia, the fear of new things.

---

106 Ibid.
107 Brené Brown, *Braving the Wilderness* (New York, Random House, 2017).

The result is that humans are adaptable and flexible. Tension between oppositional forces may feel uncomfortable, but it can also be powerfully generative. It's the tension and opposition that often reveal what is true and what matters.

Other examples of powerful paradoxes include:

FIERCE AND KIND

After the 2016 elections, I found myself thinking about what it meant to succeed as a woman. I was thinking about the kind of success that was permitted by the men who ran this country and my firm. Frankly, the antipathy hurt. As an analyst practiced at identifying linguistic trends in social media comments, I couldn't miss the trend of unconscious judgments when it came to female politicians. Mean comments about appearance, shrill voices, and straight up logical fallacies—the "double bind," that false dichotomy between likability and competency, was on full display and it made my heart sick.

I thought about natural environments where females were permitted to be strong and thought of mama bears and lionesses. I found the term "the mama bear effect" in Adam Galinsky's TED talk on the double bind. Another Adam, Adam Grant, also writes about the use of "agency" as a negotiation tool, when women identify who they are advocating for as a way to gain permission to be assertive. This is not true only for women; anyone with low status and low power is well advised to shift from a "you and me" orientation to focusing on the "we" and community.

EXTRINSIC AND INTRINSIC NEEDS

"Bill Gates argues at the World Economic Forum, 'there are two great forces of human nature: self interest, and care for others,' and people are most successful when they are driven by a hybrid of the two."

—ADAM GRANT, *GIVE AND TAKE*[108]

Two books, *Drive* by Daniel Pink and *Why We Work* by Barry Schwartz, are super accessible books on motivation. What both these books unpack is how we are motivated by both external motivations like money, prestige, power, and internal motivations like purpose, opportunity, and curiosity. When these two motivational forces are aligned and work together, we get exponential returns.

Unfortunately, we often ignore long-term intrinsic motivations and in the process end up disrupting our creativity, drive, and energy, which results in diminished returns. Essentially, we miss our chance to shift from grit and the chance to pivot into flow.

SUPERIORITY AND INSECURITY

Amy Chua writes about the tension between a feeling of superiority and insecurity in her book *The Triple Package*. She writes that one reason Asian Americans are conventionally successful is that they feel both superior and insecure, like underdogs, and have a working-class need to prove themselves. In the short term, this tension generates motivation,

---

108 Adam M. Grant, *Give and Take* (New York: Viking, 2013).

especially as young adults early in their career are motivated to prove themselves. When this energy and drive is combined with impulse control and an understanding that "a life devoted only to the present—to feeling good in the now—is unlikely to deliver real fulfillment," that power can be channeled and harnessed for the greater good.[109]

GIVE AND TAKE

Adam Grant writes about how the most successful folks are givers who think about both themselves and others. They are what Grant terms as "other-ish." High performing givers look for the win-win, concluding that games where one party wins at the expense of another are not sustainable.

One skill that successful, cooperative people—givers—possess to avoid being labeled as chumps is that they get really good at figuring out who will reciprocate, either because they are similarly motivated, trustworthy, or have a shared purpose. "Givers become doormats when they fail to use this fine-tuned knowledge of the difference between veneers and motives."[110]

Givers can succeed working with takers when they create cultures of accountability, transparent rules, and clear boundaries.

DIFFICULT HAPPY PEOPLE

Foster wraps up his lecture acknowledging that really creative folks can appear difficult to work with and hard to

---

109 Amy Chua, *The Triple Package* (New York: Penguin, 2014).
110 Adam M. Grant, *Give and Take* (New York: Viking, 2013).

understand. I'd venture that rigid thinkers and those motivated by extrinsic values don't understand the motivations of intrinsically motivated "weirdos."

This is the challenge with hiring and working with folks who are self-actualized and have a grasp on their internal power. William Dyer, a student of Abraham Maslow, admits that being self-actualized may present as being a pain in the butt.[111]

Self-actualized people, as defined by Maslow, are free of the good opinion of others, not attached to particular outcomes, and generally don't care to boss other people around. In modern parlance, they DGAF about status and what other people think.

This doesn't mean they don't want to do good work; they just may not respond in the ways we motivate folks in the corporate world. Their certainty and confidence can be seen as threatening, especially to cynical, stressed, burnt out leaders who expect deference.

That is what may make them *seem* difficult.

THE DISTINCTION BETWEEN AGREEABLE AND GIVING

Returning to Grant's work on givers and takers, he notes that one problem folks have is not being able to differentiate between true givers and true takers. "We tend to stereotype

---

111 Dr. Wayne W. Dyer, and Chopra, Deepak. *How to Get What You Really, Really, Really, Really Want.* (Hay House, 1998).

agreeable people, as givers, and disagreeable people as takers," yet in fact, these two things are independent of each other.[112]

	Agreeable	Disagreeable
Taker	False Giver	True Taker
Giver	True Giver	False Taker

Whether we cooperate or compete is often based on our values and motives. Our motivation and values are often below our conscious surface. When people are different from us and they don't jive with our elephant, we can miss out on forming a real connection if we don't lean into the discomfort and question assumptions.

Working with psychologically androgynous people, what I sometimes call "octopus" type thinkers, who are extremely flexible and curious can be especially challenging to understand.

If they haven't established trust, they can get themselves in trouble pushing boundaries and trigger insecurities of more rigid thinkers. Their honesty, creativity, and quickness can be seen as threatening and their sincere drive for the truth as infuriating. Because they move so quickly, they may assume others have the same level of quickness and flexibility and fail to recognize when they've left people behind. They are well served by slowing down. Leaders are best served giving octopus thinkers space and helping others see their fluid, challenging nature as a good thing.

---

112 For an interesting perspective on Machiavelli and whether it is better to be a False Giver or a False Taker, check out Jonathan's Haidt's *Happiness Hypothesis*.

ZERO SUM—IF I'M RIGHT, YOU'RE WRONG[113]

What we've learned with flow is that it's a balancing act, like a dance, conversation, or an exchange. It is a signal of mental flexibility.

The ability to approach a problem from multiple sides and to take multiple perspectives is also a sign of empathy. Empathy is the good stuff that allows us to connect and find agreement. It allows us to find collaborative non-zero-sum solutions and create lasting solutions.

Some leaders believe that they always know best. They consider questions, and being able to consider multiple points of view may be a sign of defiance or nonconformity. People with balanced approaches may be viewed with suspicion and considered untrustworthy and slippery.

In the abstract, this may seem absurd, but trust and safety are often felt on an intuitive level. Without mindfulness, our unconscious elephant often demands proof of safety.

Who Do We Trust?

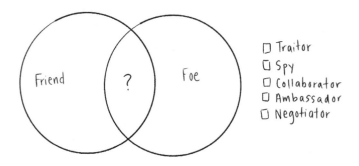

□ Traitor
□ Spy
□ Collaborator
□ Ambassador
□ Negotiator

---

113 Or "if you're right, I'm wrong, and I refuse to be wrong."

Good leaders are aware of this tension, hold space for it, and allow for the time needed to create trust and cohesion.

HAPPINESS, BUOYANCY, AND ENERGY GENERATION

This psychological androgyny, pulsing between yin and yang, positive and negative, also fits with the research on psychological buoyancy. Coming from a working-class background, the terms "good vibes only" annoys me. It feels insincere and more than a little privileged.

So, I dug into the research on positive psychology and I found that the research seems to suggest that it's actually

GOOD VIBES MOSTLY

I came across the term "buoyancy" in the works of Daniel Pink, which he derived from the research of Barbara Frederickson of the University of North Carolina, a leading researcher of positivity. I particularly appreciate it as a nuanced, research-based rebuttal to what feels like a delusional positivity brigade. Instead of "good vibes only," it's more like "good vibes mostly." According to the research, there is a range for optimal energy maintenance. It is somewhere in between three and eleven positive thoughts for every negative thought.

Psychological Buoyancy

"Positive emotions include amusement, awe, compassion, contentment, gratitude, hope, interest, joy, love, pride, and sexual desire. Negative emotions include anger, contempt, disgust, embarrassment, fear, guilt, sadness, and shame."

—DAN PINK, *TO SELL IS HUMAN*[114]

According to Barbara Frederickson, negative emotions evolved to narrow people's vision and focus our behavior toward survival. Conversely, positive emotions open us up,

114 Daniel H. Pink, *To Sell Is Human* (New York: Riverhead Books, 2013).

making us more receptive and creative. Positive emotions seem to help us with divergent thinking, and negative emotions help with convergent thinking. Since we have a bias to focus on problems, leveling the scales and being very intentional about giving our attention to positive and productive tasks makes a lot of sense.

I was discussing this with one of my clients, a former helicopter pilot and electrical engineer, and he confirmed that, at least from his perspective, it made sense. Our physical energy functions like electricity. All energy pulses between positive and negative, and functions and flows very much like water.

Some folks feel like choosing what we give our attention to, directing our elephant away from certain stimuli, is inauthentic. It may feel like we are ignoring the things that matter to us and that we don't care, like, for example, turning off the news when we feel overwhelmed or depressed.

We may feel guilty or ashamed for setting boundaries. If we don't feel guilty, there are other people who feel entitled to shame us for setting boundaries.

Part of this process is actively taking control of our energy and our attention, actively choosing what we think about. To be effective, we need to maximize our energy and protect ourselves against burnout.

Since only we know how we feel, only we can manage our energy.

COMING FULL CIRCLE

"I hold two competing thoughts in my head all the time. One is that I'm just so frustrated and angry that we've built a society where women have less money than men. I'm energized by that anger and driven by it. That's half of my brain. The other half is like, how fun is this? Seriously! I walk through airports with my Ellevest bag and young women stop me and say, 'Do you work at Ellevest? You're changing my life.' That happens all the time, and it's amazing. And to be able to build a company where I want to work, and where I would have liked to work when I was younger—it's so much fun. So I'm pissed off and grateful, simultaneously, and I'm ignited by that."

—SALLIE KRAWCHECK [115]

Let's unpack that. Anger is the emotional response people have when they feel that some form of injustice exists.[116] In this context, the negative emotion, specifically the fixation on the problem keeps Sallie Krawcheck grounded, anchored, and focused. If she only had her anger, I'd expect that she'd burn out.

Which is why on the other hand, she holds onto her joy, the gratitude and awesome responsibility she has in helping others. She is buoyed by love and appreciation, and that awesome responsibility is the fuel for moving forward.

She's a warrior who knows who she is fighting for.

---

115 Charlotte Cowles, "The Motivating Power of Staying Pissed Off," *The Cut*, October 23, 2019.

116 Brené Brown (host), "Dr. Marc Brackett and Brené on 'Permission to Feel,'" *Unlocking Us*, April 14, 2020.

When we are at our best, we hold space for the light and dark, the good and the bad, in the right proportion.

It's messy and fluid and ever changing. It's in that messiness—the active work of finding balance, negotiating it, surfing it, and learning how to articulate it—that we come to understand ourselves.

It's in doing the work that we build confidence and learn to trust ourselves and other creative weirdos who are also willing to negotiate through the twilight, the pivot, and the transition. As creatives, we must keep dancing around our center, playing both sides, all sides, and creating a new and gorgeous balance in this strange and fluid integrity.

CHAPTER TWENTY

FLOW BY DESIGN

___

This will be the shortest section of the book, but also the most important.

This is the part where we put this book down and take action.

In 2013, when I began using human-centered design, I talked about corporate design thinking with my good friend and former teammate Rafe Steinhauer, who is now a visiting professor of design thinking at Tulane University. At the time, he was involved with managing the design thinking program at Princeton University. Princeton, New Jersey, is not exactly on the route between Brooklyn and my hometown of Arlington, Virginia, which is just outside DC, but is close enough for a scenic detour on a beautiful spring day.

Over lunch, he commented that there were many good tools for teaching the beginning phases of the design process: data gathering, problem definition, ideation, empathy interviews, and so on.

However, he was in the middle of teaching the "implementation" phase and found that it was messy, broader, and much harder to systematize. This makes sense. Doing new and creative things is, by definition, not routine.

All that is to say, implementation is messy—embrace it.

START WHERE YOU ARE

You may wonder, "where else would I start?"

When I go on a diet, sometimes I wait to "officially start" until I've lost a few pounds. I'm too embarrassed to put my actual weight into a stupid app no one else will ever see. I call this "as soon as" thinking.

I realize this is bonkers. I share this tidbit so if you are similarly irrational and inclined to start not where you are but where you think you should be, I encourage you to give it up. Also, I hope it makes you feel a bit less like an oddball.

Grab your calendar or journal and start to track your energy and feelings throughout the day. You can do this in real time after each meeting, or as part of your beginning and end of the day reflections.

The first time I did this exercise, I simply went down my calendar, which I keep in a bullet journal, and drew a happy face, star, or frowny face next to each activity. Eventually, I found that the good folks responsible for *Designing Your Life* had a much prettier version called the "Good Time Journal—Activity Log," which I encourage everyone to Google and download.

We can also use our activity tracker to fill out our own flow compass and compare it against the models in the shape of emotions. Go to www.matagi.me/AFtheBook for templates and resources.

If meta-awareness and understanding emotions is a new practice, stay here for as long as is needed. Having a richer emotional vocabulary can help us understand what we believe, manage our energy, and make better decisions.

USE THE MATCH QUALITY CHART AS A COMPASS

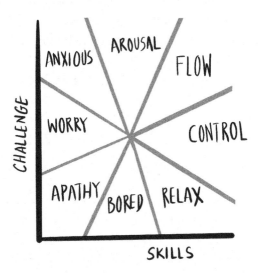

As discussed previously, most people indicated they want to be in the upper right side of the match quality chart. When we notice that some of our feelings are not what we want—for most folks that includes feeling worried, anxious, bored, apathetic—we can experiment with making a shift.

HOW ABOVE THE CURVE FEELS

When the challenge is greater than our skill—when we are over challenged or feel underprepared or unready—many people describe this feeling as stress, frustration, anxiety, and worry.

Worry is an inefficient use of our energy. If we feel worried or if we are working with folks who are always worried, take a deep breath and get clear on what we are feeling. The following are some reasons for feeling worried or anxious:

- Maybe we feel like we are pouring money down the drain either on a project or personally. Financial uncertainty is a common source of stress. It may help to get clear on our risk appetite and work within those bounds.

- Maybe we are in over our head and don't know how to ask for help.

- Maybe we see more risk than others do and are not being heard.

- Maybe a family member, or someone else we cannot control, is making bad decisions and we are frustrated.

Stress is our body's short-term kick in the pants to make a change. Its function is to get us to take action quickly so that we can get back to relaxing.

USE THE IDEAS IN THE FLOW LIST TO FIND WAYS OF SHAKING THINGS UP

Some examples may include:

- Identify what unknowns are causing the stress and do your due diligence.

- When things feel risky, get curious and clarify underlying assumptions. We may find that our teammates know more than we do. Or it may be that we know more than they do and by staying calm and communicating our concerns and clarifying the assumptions we have saved the day!

- Ask this question posed by master coach Marshall Goldsmith: "Am I willing at this time to do what is necessary to deal with this problem?"[117] We don't always have the energy or the bandwidth to solve all our problems at once. Make the best decision possible. If it really was the wrong decision, learn the lesson and move on. Make like Ariana and practice thank u, next!

- Finally, thinking back to the Leslie Odom, Jr., example, put frustration to work! Look for ways to channel anxiety productively. Practice more, get better feedback, get curious about the process and the perspective of "customers." Figure out what people need and provide it.

Finally, consider getting a coach, reading a book, taking a course, or asking for help to get what you need.

---

117 Marshall Goldsmith, *Triggers* (New York: Currency, 2015).

NOTICING HOW BELOW THE CURVE FEELS

When the challenge is less than our skill to channel it—when we are under challenged and overprepared—many people describe this feeling as one of low energy, boredom, and lethargy.

It's like planning for a large party and only having a small fraction of people show up. Many of us would consider this a total drag. When that happens, we may need to seek new ways to fill up our cup and seek new challenges.

Note: filling up our cup rarely includes busy work. Some managers do this by reflexively assigning busy work to fill up the time. Our time and mental energy is valuable and shouldn't be wasted. Sometimes time is better spent relaxing than with busy work.

Declining to take on the undervalued, underappreciated, low-valued, and unnecessary does not mean we are insubordinate or not a team player. Feelings of being undervalued and underappreciated may be perfectly reasonable. Especially if we are being told we have to "pay our dues" while seeing the reality that not everyone does. That's when clarity and documentation can be our best friend.

THINGS TO DO WHEN WE'RE UNDER THE CURVE

- Look for ways to automate the scut work. Pitch it as a business solution for the whole team or share your lessons with peers. Offer to teach these time-saving hacks through a training or lunch and learn. This will not only provide an opportunity to practice new communication skills, but it will demonstrate our collaborative values.

- Review the Flow List for meta-skills to practice. Dig into the resources in the Appendix and put them into work. Protecting our time and energy is part of our job!

- Don't neglect friendships, even when we feel overlooked. Practice sincerely celebrating other people's successes. It is actually a great pick-me-up and helps us get out of our head. When we feel low and ashamed, we tend to close off and hide. Instead, we can use that feeling as a trigger to ask our awesome friends for advice! When we ask for advice, it makes others feel connected and they may have good ideas. While we are at it, we can be a good friend in return. When we help others, we get out of our head, reaffirm our value, and often learn skills that will benefit us in the long term. Not to mention we are building buckets of trust!

- Use underutilized time to create new opportunities that only we can control. Perhaps it's creating a design and posting it on Redbubble or Etsy, or perhaps it's taking a new class. Get creative and experiment!

- Consider hiring a coach or seek out a mentor, someone who is farther down your path. Finding this person takes time. Start by inviting people out for coffee and get to know them. Be patient and enjoy it—finding our people is the journey of a lifetime.

THE THIN LINE BETWEEN ANXIETY AND EXCITEMENT

One common "trick" that a lot of coaches teach is to shift our perception of the feelings of anxiety into excitement. This makes a lot of sense, especially when we look at the match quality graph, since anxiety and arousal are at the same "challenge" level, only varying by skill. Skill, as we know from the research on grit, is talent multiplied by practice.

SWINGING BETWEEN ANXIETY AND BOREDOM

A lot of folks tell me they feel both anxious and bored, either both at once or they swing back and forth between the two feelings. This is exhausting and leads to a feeling of being stuck. Maybe we've accepted that our organization won't change and we need to find a new job. We are in a weird liminal space, bouncing between the boredom of doing a job that no longer suits us and the stress, anxiety, or frustration of not knowing what's next.

In other words, instead of getting into the pulse of flow, our feelings are swinging quickly, either too much or too little, both underwhelmed and overwhelmed. Bouncing between anxiety and boredom is like a tachycardic heart, pulsing so rapidly there is no exchange of oxygen. Without a jolt or some other intervention, the heart arrests. Similarly, without a change in situation or mindset, alternating between stress and boredom can result in burnout.

This feeling of disengagement and burnout is so common, even among our leaders, that we believe it's "normal."

It took me a while to figure out that this was not okay and to decide that I deserved better. That said, I'm still not as stubborn as *some* people (you know who you are). We need to apply our tenacity to being happy as much as we do to simply enduring.

Endurance does not equate transformation.[118]

—MARIAH IVEY, POET GODDESS

DESIGN CANVAS

We don't need to be super formal or follow an action plan. However, if it helps those of us who are perfectionists, feel free to go to www.matagi.me/AFtheBook for a list of resources and tools to put these ideas into practice, including checklists and a flow experiment canvas to help identify a problem and action plan using human-centered design tools.

NOTES ABOUT TRYING OUT THESE SOFT SKILLS

Growing up in the '80s as a latchkey kid without a cell phone, I spent a lot of time waiting around. At the bus stop or playground, there would be epic verbal battles with kids busting on each other back and forth. Part posturing, part comedy hour, the coolest kids could whip out comebacks with all the wit and timing of a Machiavellian courtier.

I was not one of the cool kids. I have never had any chill. When I did come up with a comeback it was always way too late.

Fortunately, when it comes to creating space for flow, it's never too late for a comeback. Noticing missed opportunities to be awesome is part of the practice.

---

118 Mariah Ivey "Spoken Word Poetry by Mariah Ivey," *TEDx Indianapolis Women*, November 2018.

Sometimes we recognize opportunities well after the fact. When we do, we can do a micro-assessment, asking how it might have gone better if, for example, we had stayed open and curious a minute longer.

We may even begin to notice the universal conspiracy to get us to slow down, offering us opportunities to practice patience and empathy from "idiot" drivers on our commute, to "difficult" co-workers and clients, to "impossibly stupid" bureaucratic websites. Each of these annoyances provide us with opportunities to pause, breathe, and practice mindful presence.

When we react quickly and automatically, we often don't notice or question when we swallow these toxic feelings of anger and frustration or even how we spit them out and spread them. The good news is when we do notice them in time, we can transform that poison and use the space and reflection to, with a nod to the incomparable Missy "Misdemeanor" Elliot, flip it and reverse it, sending compassion, love, and solidarity into the world.

Pausing and taking a breath, we can take our mean-spirited reactions and transform them.

For example:

- I remind myself that there is a whole story I don't know with rude drivers on the highway. Maybe she really has to go number two—who hasn't been there?

- Maybe that frustrating coworker is dealing with an illness and is just doing the best they can.

- Perhaps the website is in the process of being updated or is experiencing unprecedented surge because of sky-high unemployment levels.

Both by nature and nurture, I am not a patient person, so believe me—if there was a way to avoid being patient, I'd have found it. While we may enjoy going fast, it's better to go at the right speed. Being deliberate and patient makes it easier to endure the grit and find our flow.

RESPECT MURPHY'S LAW

When dealing with specific problems, we should be aware of Murphy's law and the fact that the universe is a sardonic son of a B. I've seen this happen a lot after a workshop when folks are excited to apply their new super chill communications and mindfulness superpowers.

One executive was excited to use these tools with what she termed a "Johnny Come Lately," who liked to throw a wrench into every project at the last minute. She was all set to practice her mental judo, to calmly transform this person's disruptive input. Instead, Johnny was focused on another project for six months and, without warning, dropped a wrench where it didn't belong.

"I can't believe I keep letting him do this," she told me, after a terse and frustrating exchange. Fortunately, she was able to recover and, with a softer heart, she went back to clarify both the team's decisions and demonstrate how his feedback was addressed and was even able to sincerely thank Johnny for his feedback. A few weeks later, after shipping the deliverable, she had a candid conversation explaining her feelings and apologizing sincerely for her initially short reaction. To her amazement, Johnny not only accepted her apology but also said he could understand how she felt and that he'd been mistaken when he had failed to respond to the earlier notifications she had sent.

"Honestly, I can't believe that happened," she said. "It feels like a huge weight has lifted from our relationship. I now actually seek out his advice instead of avoiding him."

Sometimes, it all begins with awareness of the problem.

"YOU BEST RESPECT MY AUTHORITY"

When we are experimenting with changing behavior as a peer or with a leader that is oblivious, unaware, or even resistant, we much be gentle with ourselves. Leading without direct authority is challenging and, frankly, does not always work.

Establishing trust, boundaries, and cooperative models is easier when the person with the most perceived authority sets the tone, like a boss, parent, or an older sibling. Even then, if the other person has been "burned" before, it may take more time to create an emotional safe place.

SOLID ASSUMPTIONS

Below are three assumptions that I encourage everyone to make:

ASSUMPTION 1—WE CAN ALL BE BUOYANT

Have you seen American Gothic, the painting with the stern-faced pale couple with a pitchfork in front of a barn? I've always felt like those are my people. As I've said, some of us were raised thinking happiness is a luxury. Growing up, happiness wasn't modeled in my home.

It felt like only rich, elitist, skinny, blonde people from happy families and people who were already happy would preach the gospel of positivity. They're the ones that post on social media to look on the bright side of life. What a bunch of smug jerks, I'd think. They haven't suffered, they don't know my pain.

That may have been true, but I didn't know their pain either. In the end, it doesn't matter.

If you are reading this, you have not objectively suffered the MOST in human history. In the grand scheme of things, we were born at a time where we all have a lot to be grateful for.

When we are happy and appreciative, it has a positive impact on everyone around us. We're nicer, and folks not only think we're less of a jerk, but nice people are genuinely happy that we are happy. The more time we spend denying and refusing to believe that we can be happier, the longer it takes to get to work.

We can choose to be happy and satisfied, imminently grateful for life, and still be discontented with systemic problems. Our suffering defines us only as much as we choose. It can either be the reason we fail or succeed.

I think it's an easy choice.

ASSUMPTION 2—WE CAN ALWAYS BENEFIT FROM A BIT MORE ACTION

Anyone who has made it to this part of the book is a lifelong learner. Congratulations, weirdo, you are an exceptional and rare breed! That said, ideas without action are just dreams.

We may *know* about biasing to action, but we really do need to put down this book and just do it. Find a buddy, or even create a tribe of troublemakers to make stuff up and create a new reality! That said,

ASSUMPTION 3—WE HAVE TO PACE OURSELVES

That feeling of inspiration is your flow and energy rising to the challenge! Still it helps to pace ourselves and build up our skills and talents to harness that energy.

I've done the thing where I've tried to adopt ten new habits at once. It doesn't work. Remember, this is a lifelong practice.

SMALL SHIFTS, BIG HABITS

Trying to adopt all the ideas at once can be overwhelming and may lead to discouragement. Below are some small changes that transformed my life.

2012—Journaling. I started a Tumblr, writing every day before moving to a journal. For a while this was also my mindfulness practice. It was especially helpful when I was dealing with stressful situations at work. In 2014, I also started to write three things I was grateful for each day to balance out all the negative stuff I was dumping out.

2014—Regularly practice yoga. I started to practice more and teach yoga, which is such a humbling way to deepen our practice.

2017—Started meditating twice a day. I finally started to crave that stillness of not thinking. I started making the time, first five minutes in the morning building up to about twenty minutes and eventually twice a day. I tried a few types and still flow back and forth between guided meditation, just breathing, and practicing a mantra. When waiting or walking, sometimes I use that as a chance to sneak in some bonus spaces to chill.

2017—Slow down and practice the pause. From there I noticed that my emotional reactivity shifted. I could observe my feelings and choose my response. I also started to appreciate my "wins" more deeply.

2018 - 2019—Appreciate and Reflect. One of the things slowing down showed me was that the people I loved did not know what I saw in them. They did not feel my deep appreciation, in part because I thought it was so obvious. I assumed they knew. I took my written gratitude practice and started to communicate it, sharing my reflections and understanding with the people I loved.

This took time but did not feel hard. It helped me to

GET UNSTUCK

A lot of little decisions and habits lead to feeling stuck and trapped. A lot of those decisions were made unconsciously, going with the society and/or what other people told us to do.

When we feel stuck, we can embrace the power of small shifts and unwind those decisions. We may think of our energy like a rope that has gotten twisted, kinked up, and balled up into knots. We often keep hustling, pulling it tighter, and hoping it will magically work itself out. Perhaps we imagine a big magical shift, like Alexander slicing the Gordian knot in half. If it doesn't work out or we don't have a metaphorical sword handy, we do have other options.

The Shawshank Redemption is a great example of how perseverance and taking small actions can lead to an impossible escape. If someone told us with 100 percent certainty that the only way to achieve our dream was to grind away for twenty years and crawl through "five hundred yards of shit-smelling foulness," we'd do it.

In fact, I bet most of us would start today.

QUESTIONS, KEYWORDS, AND FIREFLIES

"Judge a man by his questions rather than his answers."

—PIERRE MARC GASTON DE LÉVIS,

DUKE OF LÉVIS (OFTEN ATTRIBUTED TO VOLTAIRE)

Writing in the 1800s, Pierre had no way of knowing about Google and our ability to instantaneously answer many questions. It's no longer important that we have the answer—what's more important is that we stop to ask the question.

Einstein put this idea another way. "If I had an hour to solve a problem and my life depended on the solution, I would spend the first fift-five minutes determining the proper question to ask, for once I know the proper question, I could solve the problem in less than five minutes."

This book isn't about the answer. It is about asking the right questions and taking ownership of the way the question is defined.

How we create flow, meaning, and humanity is as unique as our fingerprint and as ever changing as the sea.

I suspect if Pierre was writing now, he might comment that we don't even need the question, you just need the approximate spelling of the keyword and Google will supply the question.

FLOW BY DESIGN · 259

In a way, the Flow List is a cheat sheet, a bunch of keywords that I hope come to mind and cue us to slow down and ask for what is needed to find flow.

CONCLUSION: WE ALL DESERVE FLOW

We deserve to be happy. Not only do we deserve to be happy, we have an obligation to be happy.

Unhappy, burnt out, dehumanized, and bullied people feel powerless and scared. This can often make them act like insecure bullies themselves. A lot of people are like that, and it's easy—and sometimes necessary—to reflect that back at them.

Elle Woods, from the movie Legally Blonde, said it best: "Happy people just don't kill their husbands; they just don't."

Legally Blonde, like its heroine, may seem like a frivolous reference, but it illustrates the importance of including diverse perspectives. In this case, it was the elitist, cynical, know-it-all Northeast establishment, who excluded the pink, optimistic, and generous point of view.

From my perspective, as another nontraditional, Ivy League voc-ed grad, there were things I've always known intuitively. Things that are obvious from my perspective as a woman, creative, quantitative nerd, and sci-fi nut and from my working-class background. My teachers and leaders didn't understand me or my flow. It took me a while to realize that they didn't understand what I—and people like me—know at our core.

FLOW IS HUMAN AND POSSIBLE FOR EVERYONE AT EVERY STATUS LEVEL

Be curious about what makes us unique and how we tick. Our job as leaders and humans is to channel and nurture, rather than to block or try to control flow.

To do this we need empathy, perspective, and kindness. We need to appreciate and include everyone.

The world wants us to be awesome. Who are we to deny that?

WHY I WROTE THIS

———

Well, that got weird. I guess I knew it would. I mean, what was I thinking trying to cram yoga, mindfulness, emotional intelligence, organizational psychology, game theory, economics, storytelling, and real-life challenges with status and inclusion and OMG, did I really talk about love and feelings in a business management book?

Holy crap.

This book, like me, is a bit MUCH.

What can I say? I'm curious about weird, uncomfortable things. I've also been frustrated by systems and companies that allow leaders—the folks with money and power—to ignore fundamental truths about people. I recognize that for some leaders, it's not comfortable to question a system that works for them. I get that.

Still, I am encouraged by the trend I am seeing with younger leaders. They don't want to be a**holes and, more importantly, don't want to accidentally encourage middle managers to be jerks or block the flow of emerging talent.

Finding a balance is messy. This book is just a draft. I considered playing it safe. I really do know how to write in a way that won't offend anyone. I wrote bland corporate copy and thought leadership for over a decade. I can be polite and play nice. But playing by the rules gets us nowhere. I also don't think writing that story would be particularly helpful or honest.

I also thought about stripping out my own story, taking out the attitude, frustration, and pain.

Selfishly, I don't think that's what I needed, as a writer working to find and create the language to write this, or what my younger self would have wanted.

I've chosen to leave out specific details for three main reasons. First, I don't have any interest in shaming anyone—shame is rarely instructive. Second, death by a thousand cuts is painfully boring to read. I'm not building a legal case here. Finally, I don't need to prove my pain for it to be real or to connect with others. I didn't write this for the folks who don't believe that bias is real. I'm not sure a book can do that.

I wish I had a magic bullet to offer you rather than this messy, intuitive practice. I don't think that's realistic.

We are all at different places, with different skills in different contexts. This ambiguity may frighten some, but I hope it fills you with joy and courage, knowing that you can figure out your own balance and create a path forward for you and others.

Having unique knowledge often feels lonely. I learned this lesson in college, first in the pages of W.E.B. DuBois and later echoed by Carl Jung and really every pioneer who has ever worked to expand our collective human understanding.

This deep knowledge and understanding can feel lonely. Knowing your truth, especially if it's something that your community denies, is painful. When leaders thoughtlessly choose to exclude people for their truth, we hurt both the folks being excluded and those who must bear witness and we teach our community that truth is threatening and less valuable than conformity.

Our deepest pain is often a signal of our greatest need. Be grateful for it. Use it!

To quote Gloria Steinem, the truth will set you free but first it will piss you off.

Here, at the end, I'm okay with that.

ACKNOWLEDGMENTS

Writing a book, much like reading a book, is a journey. It changes us. For most of my life, I've had a hard time trusting other people enough to ask for help. I'd only accept small favors. Ironically, my fear of being needy and of accepting help cut me off from receiving the trust, love, and support of those I loved. I was so intent on proving myself that I ignored those people who recognized me and accepted me just for being me. It's a crap way to go through life and one I do not recommend.

I needed a lot of help to finish this book. Editing, reviewing, encouragement, feedback, beta readers—this was more work than I realized at the start.

Here at the end, when it's just us left, I can admit I used to roll my eyes at schmaltzy, sentimental, hashtag grateful comments from other people. I didn't believe anyone could be so sincerely cornball happy. One thing I've learned from the research is that cynicism, insecurity, and being a jerk are results of burnout and trauma. Enduring bullsh*t brings out our worst, most ungenerous selves, and life is too short to be a jerk. Happiness is a choice.

This journey helped me heal, both in the writing and sharing. It helped me open up, be happy, and reconnect with my own flow. I can honestly say now I don't give a f**k if other people think it's totally cheesy when I tell you I am so freakin' grateful for everyone who helped me through this process. From the folks who threw in bucks to the book campaign, to the folks who shared their stories, to those who picked up the phone when I called and said they believed in me. You are awesome. Thank you.

Thank you, Mihaly Csikszentmihalyi, for the original research that forms the base insights for the Flow List and compass.

Mom, Dad, Daniel, Kevin, Mike, Pam. Thank you for being exactly who you are. I love you to pieces.

Thank you, Susan, for the amazing 11th Hour review and and to Dave for coming through with the 11:52 p.m. review that gave me the confidence to ship this.

Thank you, Christine Adamow, for the kick in the pants to share my research and put it into a book.

To Peter Madigan, Michelle Mahony, John Korber, Masha Sharma, Jennifer DiMotta, Sela Lewis, Lynn Borton, Sherean Miller, Robin and Michael J. Sullivan. Thank you for sharing your stories and your friendship.

To Anastasiya Plachta, Eric Koester, Shadi Abouzeid, Joshua Twilley, Siddique Essa, Beth Wolfe. Brandon Dube, Janelle Welch, Mary Glickman, Ann Senechal, Rashmir Balasubramaniam, Charles King, Courtney "MF" Kelly, Christina Schultz, Leslie Tomlinson, Bosco, Sara Zuba, Stacey Spencer Zargham, Justin Kratz, Jenny Hegland, Attila Kelemen, Susan Wexler, Alicia Vaz, TC Clare, Palak Shah, Jonathon Swersey, Leslie Marlo, Lillian Wasvary, Katherine Potter, Julie Sussman, Eleni Pallas, Megan Madigan, Tiroune Oates, Amanda Eckhoff, Angela "ATong" Tong, Diana "DD" Deleo, Benjamin Bartolome, Kendra Frederick, Radhika Chakravarti, Sandy Gani, Philip Chap, Jen and Adam Balukonis, Saleema Vellani, Emy Crinklaw-Bunch, Max Lamson, Christina Chang—Thank you for trusting me to finish this book and supporting my journey.

To my Dare to Lead Ladies. You have challenged and inspired me in the very best way, I hope you can see your influence in these pages.

Finally, thank you to all the folks at New Degree Press and most especially my editor and friend, Cynthia Tucker, thank you for walking this path with me.

NOTES

INTRODUCTION—TOO MUCH IN A WORLD OF NOT ENOUGH

Cowles, Charlotte. "The Motivating Power of Staying Pissed Off." *The Cut*, Octobere 23, 2019, https://www.thecut.com/2019/10/ellevests-sallie-krawcheck-on-the-power-of-being-pissed-off.html. Accessed on May 18, 2020.

Csikszentmihalyi, Mihaly. *Flow - The Psychology of Optimal Experience*. Harper Perennial. New York, 2008.

Kotler, Steven, and Wheal Jamie. *Stealing Fire*. HarperCollins Publishers, 2017.

Scott, Kim. *Radical Candor: Fully Revised & Updated Edition*. St. Martin's Publishing Group, 2019.

CHAPTER ONE—THROUGH THE LOOKING GLASS

Dyer, Dr. Wayne W. and Chopra, Deepak. *How to Get What You Really, Really, Really, Really Want*. Hay House, 1998.

Ginsburg, Ruth Bader et al. *My Own Words*. Simon & Schuster, 2016.

Schwanters, "Marcel Warren Buffett Says This Career Advice Is All Wrong. It's Like 'Saving up Sex for Your Old Age. It Just Doesn't Make a Lot of Sense'" *Inc. Magazine*, 1/28/19, www.inc.com/marcel-schwantes/warren-buffet-says-this-career-advice-is-all-wrong-its-like-saving-up-sex-for-your-old-age-it-just-doesnt-make-a-lot-of-sense.html. Accessed on May 17, 2020.

Sutton, Robert. *The No Asshole Rule: Building a Civilized Workplace and Surviving One That Isn't*. Business Plus, 2010.

Tan, Chade-Meng. *Search Inside Yourself: The Unexpected Path to Achieving Happiness (and World Peace)*. HarperOne, 2014.

CHAPTER TWO—GRIT AND FLOW

Duckworth, Angela. *Grit*. Vermilion, London, 2017.

Shapiro, Mark (host), "David Epstein on Match Quality, Burnout, & Range." *Explore the Space*. Episode 146, 8/22/2019, www.explorethespaceshow.com/podcasting/david-epstein-on-match-quality-burnout-range/

CHAPTER THREE—MENTORS AND MIRRORS

Gaiman, Neil. University of the Arts Keynote Address. 2012, 5/17/12. www.uarts.edu/neil-gaiman-keynote-address-2012

Gates, Melinda. *The Moment of Lift*. Flatiron Books, 2019.

Gilbert, Elizabeth. @elizabether_gilbert_writer. 7/25/19, Instagram www.instagram.com/p/BoV8qkuBc8p/

Odom Jr., Leslie. *Failing up.* Feiwel & Friends, 2018.

Wambach, Abby. *WOLFPACK: How to Come Together, Unleash Our Power, and Change the Game.* MacMillan Audio, 2019.

CHAPTER FOUR—AN ACCIDENTAL YOGI
Jonathan Haidt, *The Happiness Hypothesis,* (New York: Basic Books, 2006).

CHAPTER FIVE—EMOTIONS. WHAT'S THE POINT?
Klotz, Frieda, and Sigal Barsade. "Employee Emotions Aren't Noise—They're Data." *MIT Sloan Management Review,* 2019, https://sloanreview.mit.edu/article/employee-emotions-arent-noise-theyre-data/. Accessed on May 5, 2020.

Nhat Hanh, Thich. *How to Relax,* Parallax Press, Berkeley, 2015.

CHAPTER SIX—THE SHAPE OF EMOTIONS
Bock, Laszlo. *Work Rules!* Hachette Book Group, New York, 2015.

Brown, Brené (host), "Dr. Marc Brackett and Brené on Permission to Feel," *Unlocking Us,* 4/14/20.

Gates, Melinda. *The Moment of Lift.* Flatiron Books, 2019.

McCord, Patty. "HR lessons from the world of Silicon Valley start-ups" *TED,* June 2015, www.ted.com/talks/patty_mccord_hr_lessons_from_the_world_of_silicon_valley_start_ups

CHAPTER SEVEN—THE FLOW LIST

Fosslien, Liz and Duffy, Mollie West, *No Hard Feelings: The Secret Power of Embracing Emotions At Work*, Portfolio/Penguin, New York, 2019.

Kaling, Mindy. *Why Not Me?* Crown Archetype, New York, 2015.

Rhymes, Shonda. *Year of Yes*. Simon & Schuster, New York, 2015.

Suddath, Claire, and Rebecca Greenfield. "After Five Years of Leaning in, Everything and Nothing Has Changed." *Bloomberg. Com*, 2018, www.bloomberg.com/news/features/2018-03-08/after-five-years-of-leaning-in-everything-and-nothing-has-changed. Accessed on May 2, 2020.

CHAPTER EIGHT—MATCH QUALITY

DiMotta, Jennifer, Interview Washington, D.C. 3/24/18.

Gladwell, Malcolm. *Outliers: The Story of Success*. Little Brown and Company, New York, 2008, p. 204–217.

Harper, Jim. 8/26/2018. Employee Engagement on the Rise in the U.S. [online] Gallup.com. news.gallup.com/poll/241649/employee-engagement-rise.aspx. Accessed on May 19, 2020.

Kabir-Zinn, Jon. *Wherever You Go, There You Are*. Hachette Books, New York, 2005.

Lipman, Joanne. *That's What She Said*. Harpercollins, 2018.

Masters, Philip A., 2/5/1019. Practice at the Top of Your License: What Does That Really Mean? KevinMD.com. www.kevinmd. com/blog/2019/02/practice-at-the-top-of-your-license-what-does-that-really-mean.html. Accessed on May 26, 2020.

Newport, Cal. *Deep Work*. Grand Central Publishing, 2016.

Scott, Kim. *Radical Candor: Fully Revised & Updated Edition*. St. Martin's Publishing Group, 2019.

Wrzesniewski, Amy. "Managing Yourself: Turn the Job You Have Into the Job You Want." *Harvard Business Review*, 2010.

CHAPTER NINE. CLARITY

Csikszentmihalyi, Mihaly. *Flow - The Psychology of Optimal Experience*. Harper Perennial. New York, 2008, page 5.

Ocean's Eleven, directed by Steven Soderbergh, Warner Bro's, USA, 2001.

Salt, Bernard. *Beyond the Baby Boomers: The Rise of Gen Y*. KPMG International, 2007.

CHAPTER TEN—FEEDBACK

Buckingham, Marcus and Goodall, Ashley. *Nine Lies About Work*. Harvard Business Review Press, 2019.

University of Massachusetts, Boston. "Still Face Experiment: Dr. Edward Tronick." posted 11/20/08, viewed on 2/12/17. https:// www.youtube.com/watch?v=apzXGEbZhto.

Vaynerchuk, Gary. "Ray Dalio, Principles, The Evolution of Bridge-water Associates, & Meditation" #AskGaryVee Episode 275, 12/6/17. www.youtube.com/watch?v=itA-oJUTPMw.

CHAPTER ELEVEN—CONTROL

Csikszentmihalyi, Mihaly. *Flow - The Psychology of Optimal Experience*. Harper Perennial. New York, 2008.

Grant, Adam (host). "Burnout is Everyone's Problem" WorkLife with Adam Grant March 2020, www.ted.com/talks/worklife_with_adam_grant_burnout_is_everyone_s_problem.

Isengard, Sheena. *Art of Choosing*. Twelve Publishing, 2011.

Leah Beilock, Sian. "Why we choke under pressure—and how to avoid it." *TEDMED 2017, November 2017*, www.ted.com/talks/sian_leah_beilock_why_we_choke_under_pressure_and_how_to_avoid_it

McCord, Patty. "HR lessons from the world of Silicon Valley start-ups." *TED*, June 2015, www.ted.com/talks/patty_mccord_hr_lessons_from_the_world_of_silicon_valley_start_ups

Enrique Rubio Interview, 2019.

Team Tony. "6 Human Needs: Do You Need to Feel Significant?". *Tonyrobbins.Com*, www.tonyrobbins.com/mind-meaning/do-you-need-to-feel-significant.

CHAPTER TWELVE—FOCUS

Burnett, Bill and Evans, Dave. *Designing Your Life.* Alfred A. Knopf, New York, 2016, page 8

The Daily Show with Trevor Noah. "Lin-Manuel Miranda—'His Dark Materials' and 'Freestyle Love Supreme.'" YouTube, Uploaded 11/26/19. https://youtu.be/UUolojYEJFM

Forleo, Marie. *Everything Is Figureoutable.* Portfolio Books, New York, 2019.

Ginsburg, Ruther Bader et al. *My Own Words.* Simon & Schuster, New York. 2016.

Grant, Adam (host). "Burnout is Everyone's Problem" WorkLife with Adam Grant March 2020, www.ted.com/talks/worklife_with_adam_grant_burnout_is_everyone_s_problem.

Hill, Napoleon. *Think and Grow Rich.* Jeremy P. Tarcher/Penguin, 2008.

Mackay, Jory. "This Brilliant Strategy Used by Warren Buffett Will Help You Prioritize Your Time." Inc.Com, 2017. www.inc.com/jory-mackay/warren-buffetts-personal-pilot-reveals-billionaires-brilliant-method-for-prioritizing.html. Accessed on February 1, 2019.

Pink, Daniel H. *Drive.* Riverhead Books, 2009.

CHAPTER THIRTEEN—EVERYDAY LIFE FALLS AWAY

Bernard, Zoë. "Jeff Bezos' advice to Amazon employees is to stop aiming for work-life 'balance'—here's what you should strive for instead." *Business Insider,* 1/9/19.

Bowles, Nellie. "A Dark Consensus About Screens and Kids Begins to Emerge in Silicon Valley." *New York Times,* October 26, 2018.

Heath, Chip and Heath Dan. *Switch: How to Change Things When Change Is Hard.* Broadway Books, New York, 2010.

Newport, Cal. *Digital Minimalism: On Living Better with Less Technology.* Portfolio/Penguin, 2019.

Tharp, Twyla. *The Creative Habit.* Simon & Schuster, New York, 2003.

CHAPTER FOURTEEN—SELFLESS

Dalio, Ray. *Principles: Life and Work.* Simon & Schuster, New York, 2017.

Gaiman, Neil. "University of the Arts Keynote Address, 2012." *University of the Arts,* 5/17/12. www.uarts.edu/neil-gaiman-keynote-address-2012

Madigan, Peter. Interviewed at M.E. Swing's Coffee August 2019.

Mahony, Michelle. Remote Interview. 2019.

CHAPTER FIFTEEN—TIMELESS

Cummings, Tucker. "Does the Pomodoro Technique Work for Your Productivity?" *Life Hacker*, April 14, 2020 www.lifehack. org/articles/productivity/the-pomodoro-technique-is-it-right-for-you.html

Pink, Daniel H., *When: The Scientific Secrets of Perfect Timing*. Riverhead Books, New York, 2018, page 27.

CHAPTER SIXTEEN—LOVE AND CARE

Brown, Brené (host). "Dr. Vivek Murthy and Brené on Loneliness and Connection." *Unlocking Us*, 4/21/20.

Brown, Brené. *Daring Greatly: How the Courage to Be Vulnerable Transforms the Way We Live, Love, Parent, and Lead*. Penguin Random House Audio Publishing Group, 2017.

Buckingham, Marcus and Ashley Goodall. *Nine Lies About Work*. Harvard Business Review Press, 2019.

Daily Show with Trevor Noah. "Gov. Andrew Cuomo—Meeting Trump and Reopening New York | The Daily Social Distancing Show." *YouTube*, uploaded 4/22/20, https://www.youtube.com/watch?v=jyOnfK_UMV4.

Nooyi, Indra. "The Best Advice I Ever Got." *Fortune*, 2008. https://archive.fortune.com/galleries/2008/fortune/0804/gallery.bestadvice.fortune/7.html

CHAPTER SEVENTEEN—AN UNEXPECTED OUTCOME

Chodron, Pema. *When Things Fall Apart: Heart Advice for Difficult Times (20th Anniversary Edition).* Shambhala, Boston, 2016.

CHAPTER EIGHTEEN—THE TROUBLE WITH ASSUMPTIONS

Brown, Brene. *Dare to Lead: Brave Work. Tough Conversations. Whole Hearts.* Random House, New York, 2018, page 219.

Clear, James. *Atomic Habits: An Easy & Proven Way to Build Good Habits & Break Bad Ones.* Avery, New York, 2018.

Cowles, Charlotte. "The Motivating Power of Staying Pissed Off." *The Cut*, October 23, 2019, www.thecut.com/2019/10/ellevests-sallie-krawcheck-on-the-power-of-being-pissed-off.html Accessed on May 18, 2020.

Duke, Annie. *Thinking in Bets: Making Smarter Decisions When You Don't Have All the Facts.* Portfolio. New York. 2019.

Honnold, Alex. *"How I climbed a 3,000-foot vertical cliff—without ropes."* TED, April 2018. www.ted.com/talks/alex_honnold_how_i_climbed_a_3_000_foot_vertical_cliff_without_ropes

CHAPTER NINETEEN—THE POWER OF PARADOX

Brown, Brene. *Braving the Wilderness: The Quest for True Belonging and the Courage to Stand Alone.* Random House, New York, 2017.

Chua, Amy. *The Triple Package: How Three Unlikely Traits Explain the Rise and Fall of Cultural Groups in America.* Penguin, New York, 2014.

Cooper, Marianne. "For Women Leaders, Likability and Success Hardly Go Hand-in-Hand." *Harvard Business Review, April 30, 2013 https://hbr.org/2013/04/for-women-leaders-likability-a.* Accessed on December 2, 2018.

Cowles, Charlotte. "The Motivating Power of Staying Pissed Off." *The Cut,* October 23, 2019, www.thecut.com/2019/10/ellevests-sallie-krawcheck-on-the-power-of-being-pissed-off.html. Accessed on May 18, 2020.

Foster, Richard. "Prof. Richard Foster on Creativity." *Yale School of Management,* published 2/17/15, https://www.youtube.com/watch?v=cA8YMRMvvro.

Grant, Adam M. *Give and Take.* Viking, New York, 2013.

Legend, John (@johnlegend). "@IBNNNEWS human. Citizen. Taxpayer. I'm in my lane, homie." Twitter 8/14/14, 12:14.

Pink, Daniel H. *To Sell Is Human.* Riverhead Books, New York, 2013.

CHAPTER TWENTY—FLOW BY DESIGN

Goldsmith, Marshall. *Triggers: Creating Behavior That Lasts--Becoming the Person You Want to Be.* Currency, New York, 2015.

Ivey, Mariah. "Spoken Word Poetry by Mariah Ivey." *TEDx Indianapolis Women,* November 2018, www.youtube.com/watch?v=loBLdOp1sf8.

Made in the USA
Middletown, DE
16 February 2021